# The Street Kid's Guide to

# Having It All

## JOHN ASSARAF
### "The Street Kid"

With a foreword by Bob Proctor,
author of *You Were Born Rich*

THE STREET KID COMPANY
San Diego, California

# The Street Kid's Guide to

# Having It All

Published by
THE STREET KID COMPANY
3525 Del Mar Heights Rd., Suite 356
San Diego, CA  92130
www.TheStreetKid.com

ISBN: 0-9726214-2-3

Printed in the United States of America


Book design by Peri Poloni, Knockout Books
www.knockoutbooks.com

# Praise for *The Street Kid's Guide*

"If having abundance in your life is what you want . . . *The Street Kid's Guide* delivers!"

—**Robert G. Allen,** Author of the *New York Times* bestsellers *Nothing Down, Creating Wealth,* and *Multiple Streams of Income*

"This is the hottest new book on achieving your dream life! *The Street Kid's Guide* is on its way to the top of the book charts . . . get a copy today!"

—**Randy Zales,** President of Anthony Robbins & Associates®

"Easy to read and right on the money! This book is a must for anyone serious about having it all!"

—**Brian Tracy,** Author of *Victory!* and *Create Your Own Future*

"John has provided an outstanding road map to success . . . both from his own experiences and from his keen observation of other highly successful individuals. Reading and following the principles put forth is second only to having him as a personal mentor."

—**Dr. Tom Hill,** Author of *Living at the Summit* and co-author of *Chicken Soup for the Entrepreneurial Soul*

"Because of my job as a magazine editor and book consultant, I am frequently asked to read motivational and spiritual books. Rarely does a title motivate and inspire me as *The Street Kid's Guide to Having It All* has. The author is wildly successful as a result of these practices, and I believe a multitude of readers will be, as well."

—**Linda Sivertsen,** West Coast Editor of *Balance* magazine, author of *Lives Charmed: Intimate Conversations with Extraordinary People*

"*The Street Kid's Guide* is far and away the best personal development book I've ever seen. His poignant experiences breathe life through the pages, and his exercises, when thoughtfully completed, will change the way you think and focus your energy toward the successes you deserve. Don't just read it—do it!"

—**Kenneth Majer, Ph.D.,** CEO of MajerStrategies, Inc. and TEC Chairman, San Diego

"There is magic in this book—pure magic! I've never counted all the books in my personal development library (there are probably over two hundred). But I can tell you this without any doubt: I would exchange all of them, and all that I have learned from them, for *The Street Kid's Guide to Having It All.*"

—**Mike Lewis,** President of MLMIA 2000–2001

"*Having It All* is a one-stop shop with tangible tools that enable anyone to accomplish their goals and live their dreams. It's a contemporary version of what many of the masters of success have taught for years, communicated simply yet eloquently. John integrates the best of the best of success teaching in an easy-to-use format that gives anyone the tools to win!"

—**Liz Edlic,** CEO/Chair of One World Live

"John is a master on the journey of life. He gives unconditionally and is willing to take the risks most of us only dream about. This book is not only a guide, but also a man's reflection from someone who has been there."

—**Walter Schneider,** Co-Founder and CEO of RE/MAX New England, Wisconsin, Minnesota, Indiana, Atlantic Canada, and Europe

"Don't buy a book on how to get rich from an author who is struggling to be successful. John Assaraf went from street kid to success; he has been there and knows what he shares."

—**Dan Poynter,** Author of *The Self-Publishing Manual*

"John Assaraf has risen from the streets to the stars. He has a passion for YOU that lights up every page of this empowering book. In a world starving for possibilities, John Assaraf has created a feast you will never forget! Dig in now!"

—**Brian D. Biro,** Author of *Beyond Success* and *The Joyful Spirit*

# Acknowledgements

I must express my deepest gratitude and love to Bob Proctor. His research and teachings for more than forty years have touched so many lives, especially my own. He is truly one of the great masters of our time.

To my parents, Tsipora and Prosper, thanks for never once telling me I couldn't do something, and thank you for all your love and support. To my brother Marc, who has been my best friend, and to my sister Rivka, I am so proud and lucky to have the blessing of you both in my life. I love you two with all my heart. You *rock*.

For Keenan and Noah: Like a scientist, I have been amazed every day since you were born as I watch the two of you develop and grow into the miracle I know we all are. You two have boundless love, intelligence, and energy, and I thank God every day for having you in my life. You are the best!

Walter Schneider, Murray Smith, Bill Trimble, Jim Bunch, Mel Rothman, Robert May, Frank Polzler, Michael Stefonick, Maria Middaugh, Daniel Daou: If everyone on earth had only one friend as loving, caring, and kind as each of you are, we would not have wars. I love you all deeply and am grateful for the memories we've created.

Thanks to my dear friends Maureen Murray, Bill Miles, Randy Zales, and my outstanding professional editor Karen Risch for the efforts to bring the thoughts in my head into print. My heartfelt gratitude to Larry Michel for his valuable input on production and promotion, plus his unending pursuit of quality. Thanks to Peri Poloni for great design and working quickly to produce a wonderful look for the entire book. Ellen Reid, you are the "book shepherd" book shepherds recommend. Patty Aubrey, your guidance in getting this book moving in the right direction is greatly appreciated. Dan Poynter, you have my gratitude for your willingness to share your immense knowledge in book publishing. Evelyn Kwok, thanks for taking care of all the details that made it all come together.

To my teachers, some of whom I know intimately, others only through the gift of your research and teachings: Mark Victor Hansen, as I have said to you before, you have more brilliant thoughts and ideas in one hour than most people do in a lifetime. Thanks for your leadership, love, and support. Jack Canfield, thank you for your guidance, love, friendship, and intellect. Tony Robbins, you are a master and an inspiration to all of us who seek to share and teach. Thank you for raising the bar and for sharing your research and knowledge with all of us. Jim Rohn, your wisdom and practical approach to life touched my senses and heart many years ago when we first met. You are also one of the great masters. Deepak Chopra, you helped bridge the gap for us between the physical and nonphysical. Your endless commitment to teaching is greatly appreciated.

*With love, thank you all.*

There are obviously many others whom I can thank a bundle. I thank all the great men and women who through their daily lives learn and pass their findings on to humanity for the advancement of our species. It is only through this process that we progress toward a higher plane of understanding of self.

I thank God for making all that is.

# Contents

# Foreword

*I exist as I am—that is enough;*
*If no other in the world be aware, I sit content.*

—*Walt Whitman*

The wisdom of Walt Whitman expressed in that statement describes John Assaraf's life almost perfectly. Ask anyone who knows him, and they'll be quick to tell you that neither his time, energy, nor potential are ever squandered. John has taken himself from the streets of Tel Aviv to the world stage of business and industry. Despite coming from an early upbringing in war-ravaged Israel, where his childhood games were punctuated by gunshot and even bomb blasts, then moving to a tough neighborhood in Montreal, John turned away from violence and ultimately created a life of incredible strength, contribution, and love. He is a winner.

I've had the good fortune of knowing John for many years in a number of different capacities. He's been a dedicated student, trusted personal friend, and business associate. The quality I most admire about this man is that John is in charge of John. He has developed an extraordinary mental strength. He is rarely, if ever, swayed by the opinions of others, nor is his attitude ever affected by outside conditions or circumstance.

This man stays true to the course he has set, the game plan he has developed. His goals are specific, and he generally reaches them on or before the time he has projected. Focus could be John Assaraf's middle name. And, of the many lessons this man can teach you, this would be one of the most powerful.

On the surface, it would appear he had been blessed with an innate ability of being true to himself. However, those who know John well realize this is a discipline that has been developed through years of serious study.

John has learned and clearly explained in the following pages that we are all endowed with awesome mental faculties, which, when properly developed and scientifically applied, give each person the ability to express his or her uniqueness in a creative, productive manner.

I personally began studying human potential on a daily basis more than forty years ago, and for the past thirty-five years I've enjoyed sharing what I've learned through books, recorded material, and seminars I've taught around the world. This studying has made me acutely aware of the behavioral patterns I see expressed by the individuals I associate with. I can say without reservation that the author of this book literally lives what's on these pages better than anyone else I know. His dedication to these lessons has rewarded him with great material wealth, physical health, and the love of his family, friends, and all who know him.

In the vernacular, he has it all. What John has achieved in a relatively short period of time, you can duplicate by following the suggestions he shares with you in this book.

As I read the manuscript for this book, I felt as if I was in John's mind, observing his thoughts, feeling what he felt. This book is written as John lives. There's no waste; it's direct and to the point. The lessons are precise and accurate. You'll be introduced to various laws and concepts that may appear new to you and are not commonly laid out in most self-help books. However, I can assure you that these laws are ancient; in fact, they've always been here, and everyone who wins, without exception, must live in harmony with these laws. Ninety-some percent of the individuals who accomplish outstanding results are at a loss to articulate how they did what they've accomplished. Their success strategy is, therefore, not duplicable. John is to be congratulated for taking the time to do the research that has enabled him to share this information with you. I've found, from personal experience, that the understanding and application of these laws will enable you to accomplish any goal you choose to set.

Permit me to suggest that you read through this book once, merely to get a feel for what the author is sharing with you. Then return to the first page and begin to apply each lesson in your own life. Your old paradigm will try desperately to have you skip over the exercises you'll find in the latter half of the book. It will cause you to tell yourself that you'll go back later to complete them. Don't permit that to happen. John Assaraf has it all because he completed these exercises.

As you complete the exercises in this book, your belief in yourself will rise. I've found that belief is based upon our evaluation of something. As we begin to reevaluate ourselves, our belief begins to change. The various chapters and exercises you are about to encounter will cause you to take a long and serious look at who you are and what you are truly able to accomplish. The time you spend studying each chapter is an investment in yourself. This book will put you on the right road to a bright future.

—**Bob Proctor,** Author of the best-seller, *You Were Born Rich*

# Introduction

*Do or do not; there is no try.*

—*Yoda* (The Empire Strikes Back)

Sprinting from my family's apartment into the underground barracks, I heard fighter jets screaming overhead to meet enemy warplanes at our borders. That's the first time I can remember being scared, and it's one of my most intense memories. Today, all I have to do is mentally replay the sirens that blared in the city streets, announcing danger nearby, and the recollection still gives me the chills.

Back then, I was a typical, outgoing boy. I tried to climb everything in sight, threw rocks as far as I could, and ran fast to cross the finish line and beat my imaginary opponents. Yet I was living in Israel, a nation at war, so my races weren't always play. We had rehearsed the dash from our apartment to the barracks so many times that it was completely familiar, almost ordinary, but once the drill became reality, I couldn't help being disturbed by it. Who would be injured? Who wouldn't come home?

How can a five-year-old even begin to understand why someone wants to kill his family and friends? Or why his dad and uncles have to go fight the enemy? Or what an "enemy" is, anyway? I couldn't grasp it at that age, and I still don't understand why people would want to kill each other. The difference now is that I've learned why we make certain choices, how we become who we become, and more important, how we can become more.

## LEAVING DANGER BEHIND?

In 1966, my parents decided to take our family away from fear, away from danger, and far away from war. We moved to Montreal: Mom and Dad both spoke French, and Canada was a neutral country. In our new home, I didn't hear sirens anymore, and I learned it was okay to pick up anything on the ground and play with it. Before, doing so might have meant getting my hand blown off, since matchboxes rigged with explosives were more common than gum wrappers on the streets of my old neighborhood. In Montreal, I also noticed that people who looked different from one another seemed to get along and actually have fun together. They weren't fighting or trying to kill each other.

My father got a job as a cab driver. In addition to being a wonderful homemaker, my mother worked at a local department store. Neither of my parents had ever received a formal education or acquired a specialized skill; what they'd gotten instead was an education in real life. My mother, especially, had gone to the school of hard knocks, having left Romania to escape the war in Europe and traveled alone at the age of twelve to Israel.

Together, my parents worked hard to support our family. We were blessed to have food on the table and a roof over our heads. One thing we always had in abundance was love. Still, money was an issue in our house—specifically, the lack of it. Somehow, there was always too much month left at the end of the money.

So I began to work when I was eight and always had some kind of job, delivering newspapers or orders from the pharmacy, or pressing clothes at the dry cleaning store.

Soon, I joined a gang of kids who were adept at shoplifting and other small crimes. I never felt entirely comfortable with the stealing and the beatings (mostly me getting beaten up), but the allure of belonging and being accepted, coupled with clear rules for staying that way, kept me running with a bad crowd for several years. I enjoyed the perks of petty theft, of having cash in my pocket and a posse who would back me up in tough situations. That's where my life as "The Street Kid" began.

As you can imagine, my hard-working, honorable parents were perplexed and distressed. Occasionally, I would get caught, and my mother would plead with me about it. She would tell me stealing and lying were wrong, and I was always quick to admit she was right. But then she would ask me, "John, why are you doing this?"

My stock answer, "I don't know," is probably familiar to you if you have children. On some level, I did know why, yet I lacked the maturity to be able to express it to my mother: I felt less than all the other kids who had more, and by stealing what I wanted and being deceptive, I had discovered a way to get what I wanted and feel better about myself.

Mom and Dad breathed a short sigh of relief when I got a job at the Jewish community center across the street from our apartment. I worked in the gym, handing out sports equipment to the center's members from five to nine every weeknight. In addition to my dollar-sixty-five per hour salary, I received access to the men's health club. The pay wasn't the draw—my parents didn't know I still made more on the street selling drugs and stealing—

but I loved the club because many rich and successful men hung out there after work.

I received a lot of my early education in the men's sauna. (Hey! I know what you're thinking, and you can quit right now.) After work, from 9:15 P.M. till 10 P.M., you'd find me in the steamy room, listening to successful men tell tales. The discussions were so compelling that I didn't want to leave, not even to get water. There were many times when I'd go home at night, dehydrated but exhilarated after hearing these people talk about living the life my mom and dad wanted . . . the life I wanted.

Many of those successful men were immigrants who had come to Canada to claim their stake. I was fascinated as much by their setbacks as their successes. The stories of everything that went wrong in their businesses, family, and health gave me inspiration, because we were also experiencing our own family difficulties. I learned that it was normal to have challenges and that other families also went through similar crises.

One of the first lessons I learned from those men was never to give up on pursuing your dreams. **No matter what the failure, try another way; try going up, over, around, or through, but never give up.** There's always a way. They would talk about losing and making money, ill health, marital problems and infidelity, God, and a host of other things about which I could never hear enough.

The men taught me that it makes no difference where you are born, what race or color you are, how old you are, or whether or not you come from a rich or poor family. Many of them spoke broken English; some were single, some divorced; some were happily married and some were not; some were healthy and others were in terrible shape; some had college degrees and some didn't. Some hadn't even been to high school. It amazed me because I had somehow thought success was reserved for those without challenges and to whom every advantage had been given. I had thought it was for others, not for me.

I was dead wrong. Here's what I came to know: Regardless of the excuses you can come up with as to why you can't live the life of your dreams, someone out there is in a similar or worse situation and is overcoming it while you're complaining about it. **Someone out there is far worse off than you are right now, but is going after *having it all*.**

No matter what their current condition or situation, all of these men had strived and hoped for more for themselves and their families. They wanted to become more and to have more. And they did it. Who says you can't pursue the American dream in Canada?

## AN HONEST "MISTAKE"

When I found a hundred-dollar bill on the floor in the locker room one day, I picked it up and, for one of the first times in my life, I had a moral dilemma. One part of me wanted to keep it, and another part of me wanted to find the man who'd dropped it. Maybe it had been one of the men from the sauna, and how could I take from these men who had given me so much? Oh my, this was hard for me! In the past, there would have been no question as to what to do: Heck, I'd have stuck it in my pocket and not flinched. *Your loss is my gain! Finders keepers, losers weepers!*

Yet my sense of gratitude and loyalty led me to ask some of the members about the money I'd found. Sure enough, one man said he thought it might be his. You can guess what I thought about that (I was streetwise, after all), but before I could ask him to prove it, he went into the locker room, opened his locker, which was near where I had found the money on the floor, and pulled out at least a four-inch-thick wad of hundred-dollar bills. I almost fainted!

But it didn't end there. He asked me to go outside with him, and we went to his car. He opened the trunk, and for the first time in my life I was speechless. (To this day, my mother says she wishes she could have seen that.)

The entire trunk, no kidding, was full of neatly packaged hundreds. I was in awe and shock, unable even to guess how much money was there. The man thanked me and gave me twenty bucks for being honest, and I admit I felt a bit cheated as he left. I thought to myself, *What an idiot I am! If I would have just shut up and stuck the money in my pocket in the locker room, I'd have eighty bucks more than I do now. Dumb $%@^!*

It was the best so-called mistake I ever made. This one honest act on my part was the beginning of my education about how the real world operates and how to have everything you want by being totally truthful and learning the laws that control everything around you. **Everything you acquire—your relationships, connection with God, money, health—is a function of understanding the laws and principles that create them.** And I had to learn those laws from real life; I don't know about you, but I was never taught much about money, health, or relationships in school.

I can't recall the name of the man with the hundreds of hundreds, but I remember he was highly regarded by the other members. He would often say "Hey, champ!" to me when we passed each other at the gym. I always hoped he'd be there so I could say hi and then go listen to him talk about his life. He seemed to have it all, and from the discussions I was privileged to hear, he did. Even now, I wish I could find him so I could thank him for the clues he gave me about true success, as well as all the inspiration. I would also thank him for calling me champ. In his eyes, I was a winner.

## ASKING THE BIG QUESTIONS

I was fourteen years old when we moved to the suburbs. My parents were finally able to buy our first home, and we were all so excited. It had taken eight years from the time we arrived in Canada, but my parents were able to save enough money to put a down payment on a home and move us to the new neighborhood. The home was worth twenty-five thousand dollars. The down payment was five thousand dollars. My parents had saved about fifty dollars a month for eight years to get us this new life. As we left, I quietly promised myself that one day I'd go back to the community center and pay a tribute to the men, and especially the hundred-dollar-bill man, who'd opened my eyes to a world I knew nothing about.

It wasn't until about five years later that I decided to pursue that "new world" in earnest, however. In the meantime, I immediately got back into street life, peddling drugs and wondering if I'd ever figure out a way to earn a respectable living. This time, I went solo, sans gang, like an illicit entrepreneur. Although I learned a great deal on the streets that has actually been applicable in business (you'll learn more about that later), I paid the price in self-esteem. My illegal and immoral actions shaped my self-image, and for a long time I was repeatedly drawn back to criminal activities even when I wanted to break free.

One day at the community center in my new neighborhood, a stranger came up to me and whispered, "Hey, can I get some grass from you?"

This was a wake-up call for me. *Everybody knows.* It was as if my straight life, where I had been "the champ" at the community center, had collided with my crooked life, where I was a drug pusher. For weeks after that incident I swore off selling, but eventually I was drawn back into it.

Like a smoker, I quit and started again many times in my teens, and it wasn't until I was nineteen and moved to another city to start a new life that I finally left it all behind. After that, I never committed another crime, but I was left with a residue that took many years to completely eradicate. As a young man finally succeeding in a legitimate career in real estate, I had to battle beliefs such as "I'm not smart enough," "Nobody likes me," and "People are dishonest," which occasionally popped into my head or unconsciously drove my behavior.

> Experience is the worst teacher; it gives the test before presenting the lesson.
> —Vernon Law

Nothing is more important or healthier than having a positive self-image; likewise, nothing is more ultimately crippling than developing an identity as a criminal. After all, how smart do you have to be to pull off petty crime? Who likes a thug? What crook knows lots of honest people? These were difficult beliefs to shake, and disassembling that identity through methods you'll learn in chapter 4 was probably the single most important pursuit of my young life; without it, I never could have made it to where I am today.

Throughout this book, I'll be sharing with you my journey from being that struggling street kid with low self-esteem to becoming a multimillion-dollar entrepreneur, all by legal, ethical means. I'll not only share my own stories of setbacks and success—among them my thwarted basketball career, failed business ventures, two divorces, mega-successful multimillion-dollar merger, and averted health crises—but also the stories of other men and women I've come to admire for demonstrating the strength and resilience of the human spirit.

We need these examples to show us what's possible. We see versions of the good life on TV, but it's a distorted picture. Television presents such a skewed vision of the world, teasing us with things we want but never giving us a clue about how to get them. We can also see relationships on TV that are so messed up, with people killing each other, stealing, lying, and cheating. Where are the good examples? Where are the stories of happy marriages and successful families who have a sense of real life and what's important?

## REAL EDUCATION FOR YOUR KIDS

If you have children, this book should be especially important to you. You are your child's most influential and greatest resource. We've already established that TV won't give kids anything of great value: not a sense of purpose, not role models, not much at all except entertainment and a case of consumeritis. You can't rely on schools, either, to teach kids about the real world. An education does not guarantee *anyone* a bright future or income. There's too much emphasis on history and geography and other subjects, and not enough on self. This book will help you and those you love discover answers to such questions as, *Who am I? How do I create a life of abundance and contribution? How do I learn about my spiritual self? How can I become more, and therefore have more? How can I relate to others and learn communication skills to understand the opposite sex, or the same sex for that matter? What skills do I need for dealing with real life stress? How can I acquire money honestly, and how can I keep it?*

The school system is geared toward having kids listen, study, remember all they can, take tests, and pass if possible. For the most part, this is nothing but an education in memory, and this is not where our focus should be. Personal development pioneer Earl Nightingale once said, "If most people said what they were thinking, they'd be speechless." Sad but true! Most people don't think; they just play out their daily lives out of social conditioning, never questioning their behaviors or their cause. Computers are performing all the memory and computation skills we needed to have in the past. Now we need to teach people *how to think*. **We need to teach teachers how to effectively and properly program young students to have high self-esteem and a true understanding of themselves.**

This is not meant as an indictment of schools, but instead as a call to action. We need to revamp what our kids are learning by actively participating in their education, and we, as adults, need to reinvent ourselves to operate in this new world in which we have not been taught to live. I hope to help remedy that problem with this book. I will share with you what more than twenty years of my own research and application has helped me achieve. I have personally invested over half a million dollars of my money searching for the answers and techniques vital to creating a magical life.

## YES, YOU CAN HAVE IT ALL

In *The Street Kid's Guide to Having It All,* you'll get the lessons I learned and know the exact steps I took to grow from being a small-time gangster to becoming a respected and successful businessman; loving father of two; happily divorced (meaning I have a great relationship with my ex-wife), blissfully single (meaning I'm in love with my girlfriend), and genuinely happy guy. You'll be able to use my experience to enhance your life in the same way I benefited from those stories at the community center. But don't misunderstand that I think I'm different from anyone else. There are thousands of people who didn't know how, didn't have the resources, and didn't have the education, who are living life to the max with health, wealth, great families, careers, friends, and a strong spiritual connection with our Maker.

You can, too. In this book, you'll learn how to

➤ develop and utilize the seven power factors all successful people use,

➤ use the law of attraction to achieve all of your life's dreams,

➤ uncover and eliminate the mental and emotional obstacles keeping you from your true potential,

➤ use the Life Design Matrix to create the life you truly desire, and

➤ optimize street kid smarts in today's quickly changing society.

Of all the people I know personally who "have it all," not one of them was given it on a silver platter. They all decided what they wanted and then became more than they were before. They worked and studied their way to getting what they wanted.

Yet most people spend more time planning a vacation than they do thinking and planning for life. Don't be one of those people who just reads this book and puts it away, hoping things will change for the better. If you don't change, nothing will change.

It's been said that the definition of insanity is doing the same thing over and over again and hoping for a different result. Don't be crazy! Be willing to try something different. Be willing to challenge yourself to become more than you are right now.

*Experience is one thing you can't get for nothing.*

*—Oscar Wilde*

If you think this book will give you a magic trick or potion, put it down and read something else. This book will give you information for you to get your motivated butt in gear and put your mind to work on creating your own masterpiece. The steps are easy, but make no mistake: It takes plenty of learning and effort to create the life you want for yourself and those you care about.

If you truly want a better life than you have now, do what it takes. Otherwise, give yourself and those around you a break and just admit that you don't want to pay the price, that you'd rather whine and complain than step out of your comfort zone and do what's necessary to make things better for yourself. If you're committed, you'll find this process is easier than you could have imagined. If you're not, it will take longer and be more difficult than you ever thought. Choose to commit: Being on purpose has a lot of power and gives you unstoppable momentum.

Many years ago, Jim Rohn, a great inspirational and motivational leader, told me that we either pay the price of discipline or the price of regret, and discipline weighs ounces while regret weighs tons. Are you ready to pay a small price for the life of your dreams?

Let's journey together into self-discovery and amazing possibilities.

**PART I**

# The Street Kid's Secrets of Success

### CHAPTER 1

# What Is Success?

*Obstacles cannot crush me. Every obstacle yields to stern resolve. He who is fixed to a star does not change his mind.*
—*Leonardo da Vinci*

With so many different beliefs about and definitions of *success,* it seems the word is overused. Certainly, success too often refers to how much money someone earns in a year or to net worth. Of course, earning a lot of money can be wonderful. Yet there are plenty of people who have acquired great wealth only to find themselves emotionally or physically broke. Relationships with a spouse or kids have been the sacrificial lambs for money. Many have even forfeited their own health for the mighty dollar. I don't know one person who has lost good health and wouldn't give every nickel to regain it. The same is true for those who have lost a child's or spouse's love in the pursuit of financial gain and material riches.

Many people achieve financial success at the expense of the rest of their lives. They keep thinking that once they make a certain amount of money, they'll slow down and have time for other important things like family, God, and health. But most people never get there; there's always more money to be made, one more thing to do. It's usually too late before they realize that every day is the journey, and it's not just about the money. It's important to create a successful and fulfilling balance in each area of life.

One of my dear friends, Michael J. Stefonick, spent more than twenty years building a multimillion-dollar business while his marriage and relationship with his two kids suffered. Shortly after his annual physical, his doctors disclosed the results of an MRI scan of his brain. They found a large tumor that would soon cause him to go blind or kill him. When he asked for a solution to the problem, he was told surgery was the only answer; however, there was only a fifty percent chance he would make it through the operation.

Within seventy-two hours, Michael arranged to sell his company and made all the necessary other preparations in anticipation of his possible death.

After ten hours of surgery, a large and benign tumor was removed. Michael spent three weeks in the hospital, then went home for recovery, where he was nursed for several months by the very people he had neglected, his family. Today, he's doing great and working to build a successful consulting business in the same industry in which he made his first fortune. More important, he's also making sure he gives plenty of attention to his health, his kids, his ex-wife, and his true friends. Somehow, what's important becomes obvious when life is on the line.

Guess what? **Life is on the line every day, and you are trading what you do for it.** In other words, life is a series of trade-offs, and every moment is literally spent: Time and, therefore, our lives are traded for the things we choose to do.

Imagine for a moment if my friend had been you. How would you have felt and reacted? Would you have wished you could go back in time and make different decisions?

## PLANNING FOR TOTAL SUCCESS

Success can be incredibly elusive, or it can come in abundance with the right mind-set and know-how. Few people really understand how to create abundance, particularly abundance in every facet of their lives. Fewer still have studied the cause of results. As a consequence, most people have no clue as to the awesome power that resides within them. Even successful people don't really understand the true cause of their success. They can tell you what they do, but rarely can they explain why or how they do it.

Yet you can have it all, including but not limited to lots of money. Instead of realizing this, most people accept the way things are in their lives as some kind of foregone conclusion. They blame the circumstances or conditions into which they were born for the way they live today. **But the truth is, you create your circumstances and reality.** How many people have to overcome trying circumstances to create the life of their dreams?

Almost everyone who achieves success—which I define as fulfillment in all areas of life—faces difficult times. The trick is not getting sucked into the idea that those difficulties determine destiny. If I had stayed in the gang, if I had allowed my health issues to hold me back, if I had given up when I felt abandoned in business, if I had gone back to selling drugs after a series of devastating events I will explain later, if I had given up on love after my second divorce, if, if . . . If anyone had an excuse for settling for mediocrity, it would have been me. But I was lucky. I learned from my mentors that specific laws govern the universe, and specific tools can help you make the most of them. (You'll learn about these laws in detail in chapter 3.) You simply don't have to settle. God blessed you with the power to create whatever you choose in this life. The more you discover who you *really* are, the more you'll believe you can create a life of total abundance and have it all.

The more you learn about the precision and exactness of our universe and, by extension, yourself, the more you'll understand the power you have available to you, right now, to create a magical life.

## YOU CAN BE HAPPY RIGHT NOW

Like success, happiness is too often misunderstood as a function of how much money you have. Just make enough cash, and you can buy happiness. Just get this or that thing or experience, and you'll be happy. *Not true!*

I have certainly had the experience of pursuing money to the exclusion of everything else. Selling drugs was a way for me to have lots of money, but it didn't assuage my hunger to be something greater. I went through cash like water, emptying my pockets as fast as they were filled, going to the amusement park, buying gifts for friends, eating out, drinking alcohol. None of the money I "earned" and none of the material goods I bought could bring me happiness. Temporary relief and instant gratification, yes, but happiness, no.

Even after I left the streets, I still thought money would do it for me. I thought that the reason it hadn't worked thus far was simply that I hadn't had a legitimate way to earn it. So I became single-minded in the pursuit of career success, and there's no denying I excelled. Intense focus on being a prosperous real estate agent definitely paid off. Learning as much as possible from the agents who were doing well, at their suggestion I also dove into the works of Tommy Hopkins and other sales training gurus who, it turned out, always seemed to include a healthy dose of personal development training, too. Fortunate for me, along the way to earning more than I ever had—and doing it legally, with integrity—I also earned my own self-respect and expanded my personal definition of success to include much more than the acquisition of money.

In 1982, when I was twenty-one and had just made my first fortune in real estate, I took a break from work. Using my savings, I embarked on a fourteen-month trip around the world, visiting California, Hawaii, Fiji, Samoa, Tonga, Indonesia, Malaysia, Singapore, Hong Kong, India, Israel, Europe, New Zealand, and Australia. In all the time and all my travels, I never had a bad experience. Above all else, I was impressed with how generous and kind people were. In New Zealand, people would take me thirty miles out of their way just so they could talk with me, learn about me, be kind to me.

I was especially drawn in by the indigenous island cultures. Here were tribes of people living on small strips of land in the middle of the Pacific who seemed to be completely happy without the comforts we think are so important. No fancy cars. Heck, no cars at all. No television, no grocery stores, no health spas, not even a community center gym. How could it be that they had none of our materialistic possessions and yet were so content? They taught me this simple reason: **Happiness is a personal choice and not the product of anything external.**

Material things don't have the power to make you happy. They can give you comfort and enjoyment, but not happiness. Instead, you must make the *choice* to be happy. You may not like some of the events or circumstances going on in your life, but the choice to be happy is yours. It comes from the inside, so you have complete power over it and can make this choice any time.

Happiness means something different to each person. You must choose what it is to you and then create a plan for achieving it. It is not what someone else thinks you should be or have. It is all about making your own decision.

You are creating a life no matter what, so you might as well *have it all.* This book will help.

➤ You need to understand who you really are. We'll explore this eye-opening subject in the next chapter.

➤ You must understand the major natural laws that operate and govern the universe and work with exact precision. In chapter 3, you'll discover the seven major laws that affect you every day.

➤ Then you can begin to delve into why you are the way you are and why you're getting the results you're getting. Many people have never really stopped to examine their lives and their current results. But in chapter 4, you'll examine and understand exactly what caused your habits and beliefs. You'll determine which ones you still need and which ones you want to leave behind and change.

➤ Understanding exactly where you are in life now is what I call finding "true north." (There are others in my field who refer to "north" in a similar way. I'm aware of at least two authors, Martha Beck and Stephen Covey, who have built on this concept in wonderfully empowering ways. I first heard the idea twenty years ago from my cousins, who learned it while they were in the Israeli Army.) It is vitally important to be totally honest about your current results and not puff them up for the sake of ego. Chapter 5 will give you a new compass so you can choose a course more in line with exactly what you want. Regardless of what your current results are, you can improve on them. The journey involves health, wealth, spiritual awareness, family, friends, and the career in which you choose to express yourself.

➤ Perhaps the most important part of this whole deal is determining what you want from and in your life, and then developing a real plan for getting there. In chapter 6, you'll start to design the life of your dreams and get on your way to greater accomplishments.

➤ The real key here is to first design your dream life, then create a plan that will move you in that direction. It's no different from building a home. You sit with the architect, design the home you wish, and then move into action to build it. In chapter 7, you'll realize how much you are the architect of your own life and that you are totally capable of designing and living a masterpiece if you choose.

➤ In chapter 8, you'll learn the seven power factors every successful person must use to create a dream life. All these power factors are skills you can develop and use to create whatever you want.

➤ Many people have heard about visualization and meditation, yet few people use them on a daily basis. They are, without question, two of the best ways to catapult your life into calmness, serenity, and total success. In chapter 9, you'll get all the details on why and how to use these awesome techniques to help you *have it all.*

➤ In the last chapter, you'll see how faith can support you in creating the life of your dreams, no matter what your religion or practice.

Creating true success does not have to be trying, exhausting, or draining. It can simply unfold like so many other miraculous creations in our universe. Think for a moment. How hard does an oak tree try to grow? How much effort does the ocean put into the crashing waves? How much work is it for the planets to move the way they do in such perfection and harmony?

### CHAPTER 2

# You Are Not Who You Think You Are

*And now here is my secret, a very simple secret: It is only with the heart that one can see rightly; what is essential is invisible to the eye.*

*—Antoine de Saint-Exupéry*

Who are you? If I asked you this question, you might point to yourself, tapping your chest with a thumb or index finger. If I told you no, that's your body, then you might say your name. Again, an inaccurate answer. A name is given at birth, and certainly you existed before then. You existed before your parents were even aware of you.

Think for a moment about what it took to create you. Billions of years of evolution produced a sentient life form called humans. Intelligent energy continuously reproduced and grew smarter and smarter with each generation.

Then two cells came together and miraculously multiplied, generating a body and a brain that rivals any other organism on this planet. You matured into a mass of perfectly formed intelligent energy that, through your eyes, appears to be solid. Yet *you* are not a body or brain. Your body and brain, however, are parts of you.

You have to admit that for you to be here, to exist, an incredible amount of intelligence and order had to be in place and in charge of the creative force to make humans. You've probably heard before that the chances of our infinitely complex, interdependent universe having arisen from an ancient accident are about as likely as an explosion in a modern printing press producing the latest version of Merriam-Webster's dictionary. Think of it: The ingredients are there in the print shop, and then *kablooey!* The paper shoots into the air, ink squirting everywhere, metal flying, and voìla! A beautifully bound, alphabetized book of words and their definitions falls out of the unorchestrated bang. Not likely at all.

If you're partial to scientific proofs, then consider this. We live in an expanding universe; it gets bigger and bigger with every passing second. We know this from studying the nature of galaxies and observing that they grow more distant from one another as time goes on. Then what if we went backward in time? The galaxies would get closer and closer together until they finally converged at a point, at the beginning, at what scientists call a "singularity." If there was a beginning, there must have been a Beginner, an Initiater, a Maker. Otherwise, we would say that there was no cause. Possible? Perhaps. But not logical: It would defy all the scientific laws of chemistry and physics. To believe that our universe is causeless flies in the face of everything we know about our physical world.

To some, the physical world is itself evidence enough. Michael Behe, in his 1996 book, *Darwin's Black Box,* marveled at the complexity of blood, specifically its ability to clot. Without getting overly technical (a professor of biochemistry at Lehigh University, Behe uses words like *irreducibly complex, enzymes,* and *cofactors*), suffice it to say that he doesn't believe blood clotting could possibly have come about solely by way of Darwin's natural selection. Nope, Behe says, it must have been initiated by something else. It must have been *designed*. (By whom? What do you think?)

I suppose that if you don't believe in a Designer, which I am fond of calling God, this book won't convince you. **Yet I suggest you are made up of and directly connected to the Infinite Intelligence that created you.** You can call it whatever you choose; that's up to you. The important point is that you understand you are not separate from it. It is you. It is the "I" we speak of when we say, "I am."

A drop of ocean water is made up of everything in the ocean and it can never be anything but what it is, no matter how far you take it from its source. It appears to be water because that is the name we gave it. It actually is made up of two hydrogen atoms and one oxygen atom—energy in a certain and orderly state of vibration, just like you and me.

When energy is tightly bound together, it appears to be liquid or solid. If you took the water and heated it, you would turn what was liquid into steam or vapor, the elements of which are still there in the atmosphere. The same is true of the body when it dies. Whatever atoms and molecules make up the body disperse back to the source from which they came.

I liken my mind-body system to an F-16 fighter jet. The more I know about how it functions, the easier it is to fly. Many people don't have a clue about the physical and mental gifts they are blessed to have. Think about the training a fighter pilot receives to learn how to handle a fighter jet. We need that kind of training to learn to handle and maneuver ourselves.

## THE PHYSICAL BODY

The body is a marvel that functions like no machine ever created by humans. Too many people treat their bodies, their only "vehicle" in this life, as if they could get another when the first one is used up. It is imperative to understand exactly how your body operates and what you can do to tap into the world you cannot see with your eyes.

You can hear, see, taste, smell, and touch with your physical senses. Your nervous system picks up these stimuli, which your brain transforms into an "inner" understanding based on your personal perceptions and past conditioning. Your body was created to get you around like a jet, and your senses are used to gather information coming from various sources of energy in different frequencies.

Your senses have evolved greatly to get you around the physical world in which you live today. You "hear" sound, which is made up of sound waves. You "see" light waves through your eyes, and the image you see on the screen of your mind is nothing more than energy in formation. When you see something with which you are familiar, your brain analyzes the information it receives through your eyes and recognizes it from previous memory. If you don't recognize the sound or image, you say you "don't understand" what it is until you create a new reference for it in your memory bank. Your brain is able to decipher the frequencies of a multitude of sources of energy and store every experience you've ever had. It also analyzes the information, and then you make decisions based on a variety of factors such as your beliefs, habits, and conditions. Your brain is one incredible piece of equipment!

## THE NONPHYSICAL CONNECTION

You and I are pure intelligent energy in a formation we call body. The flow between Spirit, the mind, and the body is constant and creative. The study of psychoneuroimmunology (mind-body medicine) bears this out by showing how profoundly what we think and feel affects our physical health—or lack of it.

In my early twenties, I was diagnosed with ulcerative colitis, an embarrassing disease with no known medical cause, though it's clearly stress-related. The bottom line, pardon the pun, is that the large intestine gets ulcers, which cause bleeding, abdominal pain from severe inflammation, diarrhea, and a host of other unpleasant effects. You know how everyone has a "most embarrassing moment" story? Ulcerative colitis provided mine.

Back then, I thought I was a hotshot in real estate. In truth, I was an ambitious young man of twenty-two trying to look older while working to relocate high-roller clients from Montreal to Toronto. One day, I went to pick up a fellow, a bank president, in my Cadillac Sedan DeVille, which I realize in retrospect must have looked like my dad's car. Brand-new, silver-gray on the inside, it was the perfect real estate agent's car—for a forty-year-old. Although I thought I looked pretty stylish, I wasn't feeling well, since I was in the middle of a three- to four-week bout with my ulcerative colitis. Once I arrived at the airport, I had an attack: My colon was seriously swollen, I hadn't eaten much for weeks, and anything I did eat meant an explosion was on the way.

The man got into the car, and I raced away from the airport, making a bee-line for the nearest gas station, where I pulled in, jumped out of the car, and ran for the bathroom. Too late. Wearing a lovely, tailored Italian suit, I literally lost it and shit all over myself.

I ran to the bathroom, stripped off my pants and underwear and tried to clean up with paper towels in a tiny white sink.

Completely frustrated, the client came to the men's room about thirty minutes later, where he discovered me standing there in my shirt, tie and socks, butt naked otherwise. He was distressed.

"What happened to you? Are you okay?" he asked, thinking maybe I'd been assaulted.

What could I say? I let him in on my predicament and told him there was an extra set of clothes in the trunk of my car, which I kept there for just such an occasion. He brought me the bag, I changed, and we drove to my house, where I could clean up properly. Mind you, I had never met this man before, had only spoken to him on the telephone, but he was incredibly nice about the whole thing.

Nowadays, I can laugh about it, but at the time I was so ashamed and embarrassed that I felt like jumping off a bridge. I'm telling you this because I want you to understand this was a serious, unpredictable, incredibly inconvenient ailment. It was not a situation where mind over matter was an option—back then, I didn't know anything about mind over matter, and I couldn't simply "hold it" and make the problem disappear. Yet my mind was indeed where the key lay to solving the problem. I was taking twenty-five pills a day to get it under control and using cortisone enemas twice a day. This was *not* fun, especially since I was single and trying to date. For some time, I let this disease control my life, and as long as I was its victim I was miserable.

When I decided to change the outcome of this horrible sickness, I became a student of the disease, discovered how much stress played a role in my own manifestation of it, and set out to heal myself. Know that this incident at the filling station was not the only time I was mortified by my illness, so the temptation to just take something to make it go away was definitely present. But I figured that when you're in such an embarrassing situation, you can succumb to that and let it control you, or you can find out what is causing it and treat it at the cause.

I became an expert on ulcerative colitis, learning more about it than even my internal medicine doctor knew. All he could do for me was keep pushing the drugs. (Funny that someone was trying to sell me drugs for a change, isn't it?) I put myself on a strict regimen with a tremendous amount of visualization, proper eating, exercise, positive affirmations, and writing. (You'll learn specific methods for modular visualizing in chapter 9.) To remove the old programming of stress and sickness, every day I instead visualized myself as relaxed, calm, peaceful; I saw my colon healed and healthy. In sum, I set out to remake my body at the cellular level, as Dr. Deepak Chopra so eloquently puts it. After all, he tells us, the human body is constantly rejuvenating itself—liver cells regenerate in about six weeks, skin cells in only four, stomach lining cells in just four *days*, and eye cells in just two. (How amazing is that? You literally have new eyeballs every two days!) Chopra says that where disease is present, so is the cellular memory of that disease, so as cells regenerate, they perpetuate the illness. If you can eradicate that "phantom memory," as he calls it, you can also limit or eliminate the disease.

Those who are successful at healing themselves, he says, are those who can fall into "the Gap," that place where the "thinker behind the thoughts" resides. You might simply call this getting in touch with your essence. Most people don't understand this connection between the body and the source of all there is, the Intelligence that created them and is them. Most people have been so conditioned to just live with and accept that all they are is what they can see or feel. But Chopra and many other physicians can tell innumerable stories of people who were able to regain eyesight, heal cancerous tumors, and, in my case, cure ulcers through meditation and reconnection with the "higher self."

Your higher self or spiritual side is part of the universe, as is your body, whether you are aware of it or not. We now know that everything is part of everything else; it's all interconnected. **We are not separate from each other or that which created us.**

Most people think they have only to work hard to get results, but there's an easier and much more effective way to achieve your goals and dreams. When you use your body's physical ability in conjunction with the power of the universe and your higher self, everything flows perfectly as it should and does in nature. There's a perfect balance in nature when humans get out of the way. Consequently, you must learn how to get out of your own way.

Imagine that your body is a rocket ship and your spiritual side is the booster. I think you'd agree the boosters could have a significant impact on the journey. Most people are lugging around a rocket ship, and they don't know how to turn on and use their own boosters. Let's fire them up!

*The problems of the world cannot possibly be solved by skeptics or cynics whose horizons are limited by the obvious realities. We need men who can dream of things that never were.*

*—John F. Kennedy*

Your body has an operating system just like a computer does. Some of the functions are preprogrammed and controlled by what we refer to as the subconscious mind. Others you consciously control, such as choosing what to eat.

By understanding the exact functions and power these two systems have, you can allow the proper system to do the proper function. Once you start to use your gifts the way they were meant to be used, your life will flow like never before.

Let's start with the conscious part of you first. This part of you is simple to grasp, easily understood as having six intellectual functions. These are things over which you have complete control and of which you are entirely aware.

Don't be surprised if you've never heard of these functions before. How and when were you supposed to learn this vital information? As far as I know, they don't teach it in any school. This information is readily available for anyone seeking to understand the true cause of our results, yet I rarely meet anyone who has truly been a student of these principles. They are so valuable! The conscious mind's facilities were delineated for me as they are here by Bob Proctor, a wonderful teacher and mentor. Likewise, he was the first person to articulate to me the laws you'll read in the next chapter. I don't believe he is the originator of these ideas, but he is a master of distilling complex subjects into actionable principles.

---

[1] If you'd like to know more about Bob and his inspirational products and resources for developing your success, visit www.BobProctor.com. You can also receive his free insight of the day by subscribing at www.getmotivation.com/insights.html.

**Your first intellectual function is reason.** The conscious side of you makes day-to-day decisions and keeps you aware of what's going on as you're walking down the street, hitting a baseball, or sewing. Whatever choice you have to make, your conscious mind is in charge. You can choose a thought and move your body to do what you want.

No one on this earth can choose your thoughts for you. People can force you to do certain things, but your thoughts are *totally* in your control. When you choose a thought, it creates a feeling in your body. You take action and then a result is produced. No matter what the result is, an action preceded it—an action *you* chose. That is why you must accept complete responsibility for your results.

If you don't like the results in your life, you must consciously make different choices using reason, your conscious mind's ability to think and evaluate what you want and feel. If you know your ability to reason may not be your greatest asset, choose a friend or family member to assist you when serious and important decisions must be made. You'll learn more about working with a mentor in chapter 7.

**Your second intellectual function is will.** Will is your mental toughness. Without it, there's no hope of ever living a life of abundance. Your will gives you resolve when everything around you seems to be crumbling and keeps you going even when your body thinks it can't anymore.

When nine coal miners were stuck in a flooded shaft 240 feet below ground in western Pennsylvania, no doubt their will got them through the ordeal. They spent the first twenty hours just waiting for rescue work to begin, because a drill rig had to travel from West Virginia to the site. Then the giant drill bit broke when it hit hard rock one hundred feet down, and they had to wait eighteen more hours before work resumed. Because the miners were unable to communicate directly with the workers, they didn't know if the rescue team couldn't find them or had given up or who knew what. Several men scratched good-bye notes to their families, but they hung onto the hope they would get out, and their will kept them going. Ultimately, all nine men were rescued.

Seventy-seven hours in a cramped mineshaft, weighed down in the water by heavy mining clothes, could easily trigger panic in most anyone. Yet these men found the strength to stay calm enough to survive. They tapped on the walls and pipes in the mine to let rescuers know where they were. They tied themselves together to prevent losing any of the men; even if someone died, they reasoned, he wouldn't float away in the cold water. They literally kept their heads up, positioning themselves so everyone could continue to breathe despite the fluctuating water height.

It was a remarkable story of the miners' will, the rescuers' dedication, and the families' faith that their men would return alive. One woman prayed the whole time her husband and brother were trapped in the shaft. "I just knew it . . . wasn't their day," she said.

Equally inspiring, your will serves you even when your life isn't threatened. It's one of your greatest resources. Once you've chosen exactly what you want in life and begin to pursue something that is great to you, your will to do whatever it takes carries you when the times are tough.

Usually, your results in life are determined by the greatness of your will. To create a great relationship, an abundance of material wealth, glowing health, and so on, requires strong will.

Curiously, some people seem to be born with an enormous will; they'll climb mountains no matter how high they are, while others just give up. What if you think you are weak-willed and you want to change that? Find your passion, which is the genesis of will. For the men in the mine, their instinctive passion for living kicked in. In your life, the more driven you are by something, the more will you'll have for it. Find something that will charge you up, something big and exciting and not particularly easy to accomplish. Then go for it! Will develops like a muscle: the more you use it, the stronger it gets.

> You can chain me, you can torture me, you can even destroy this body, but you will never imprison my mind.
>
> —Mahatma Gandhi

**Your third intellectual function is memory.** This is also like a muscle, and some people exercise it more than others. Barring neurological or chemical problems, everyone can have an excellent memory. It's your responsibility to keep your memory strong by using it. Remember the saying, "If you don't use it, you'll lose it." Memory is all about practice and learning techniques for recalling what's stored in your brain. Memory never leaves; it just gets weaker if you don't apply it. If you suffer from a memory that isn't performing as well as you'd like, start doing some exercises to develop that side of your conscious mind. It's no different from your belly. Start doing something about it! There are numerous memory-enhancing games and methods available to you. My kids play "concentration" all the time—various versions of the game where you lay out a deck of cards face down and collect suits by turning over one card at a time and remembering where the matching ones are. You can also purchase books, tapes, and other resources designed for improving memory in adults. It doesn't really matter which one, so long as it works the muscle.

**Your fourth intellectual function is perception.** Because everyone sees the world differently based on their beliefs, habits, and conditioning, perception is kind of a wild card. Everyone interprets the world differently. People may have some similar beliefs, but their overall experience is different due to how they label and understand every event in their lives.

Those who are open to seeing and not judging have the greatest understanding of what's really going on. Observing without judgment is an art. To understand that your point of view is only one possibility in an endless realm of possibilities opens doors to another perspective. It enriches your experience when you allow another's point of view to be absorbed and pondered. So much conflict in our world comes from people's inflexibility about their perceptions. They see the world based on what they were taught and the programs and beliefs they have. Appreciating another person's point of view and beliefs would help all of us a great deal.

Next time you're confronted with something or someone you don't like, pay attention to your internal dialogue. Be aware of how you respond and react to the situation. Ask yourself, *What's causing me to judge or react this way?* By probing your own mind, you get a deeper insight into how you perceive the world. For example, the next time somebody cuts you off when you're driving, consider your response. Do you calmly let the car pass? Do you get angry and signal your ire in some way? Do you sigh and swerve, dramatizing the other car's impact on you?

Underneath your reaction, no matter what it is, lays a single question you're asking yourself. No, it's not a question about the character or skills of the other driver; it's a question about *you:* "What does it mean about *me* when somebody cuts me off?" One person might say, "They don't respect me," another person might say, "It doesn't mean anything about me; they're just driving like a maniac," and still another person might say, "People always take advantage of me!"

Examining my own reactions while driving was a great exercise for me when I lived in Los Angeles, where if I had reacted every time someone cut me off or any time I was stuck in traffic, I'd have driven myself nuts. So instead of falling into the trap of my perception, I learned to tell myself, "It's just traffic. It's not about me."

*You can't depend on your judgment when your imagination is out of focus.*

*—Mark Twain*

Once you've observed yourself in reaction to a situation, start to explore whether you are reacting to other events that are equally impersonal. Can you look at those things, too, and tell yourself that it's "just traffic"? Can you realize that all your reactions in life simply reflect one possible perception, only one possible interpretation from an infinite number of views? This is the starting point for becoming an observer without judgment.

**Your fifth intellectual function is imagination.** The imagination provides you with a great mental playground. The creative process starts in this world of possibility and exploration.

What if you were encouraged to daydream about all the wonderful things you could become and have? All creative people use their imagination to generate ideas they eventually can take from mere thought into tangible existence. Everything is first created in the mind, and then it is created in physical form. You have the ability to imagine anything you want. You tap right into all the intelligence and energy with your imagination.

Through your imagination, you can tap into another frequency of the nonphysical. The thoughts or visions in your head are just bits of energy forming an image on the screen of your mind. You can imagine anything, as others have, and create the physical equivalent of what you see. Just look around you and you'll know this to be true. All of humanity's creations and discoveries started in someone's head.

Imagination is one of the most misunderstood parts of the conscious mind. Supremely active among children, adults sometimes squash it when kids don't behave the way they want them to. Yet you should celebrate imagination, even when it doesn't look "appropriate," or "mature," or "behaved." The imagination is your direct link to the world of possibilities.

Imagine that you have an extra hundred thousand dollars with which you can do whatever you want. Imagine for the next thirty days that you have the best romantic relationship you've ever been in. Just imagine. Let yourself soar. Then be aware of the vibration of your body, of how you physically feel, what the mental uplift is, what happens to your emotions. When you imagine all that goodness, your body vibrates on a positive frequency, doesn't it? You can feel it! Now know you have the ability to imagine as much as you want—and using your imagination to repeat a thought and feeling, over and over again, creates a " conditioned program" that keeps you in that frequency at a subconscious level, so your goals and dreams are drawn to you while you are doing everything you can to move toward that desired outcome.

**Your sixth intellectual function is intuition.** Awesomely powerful when you pay attention to it, intuition picks up "vibrations" or intangible feelings that either seem right or don't. It's that feeling you get about a person even when they haven't said a word. It's that feeling you get when danger is present. It's also the feeling you get when you should act quickly and take advantage of a situation both in business and in your personal life.

A feeling is nothing more than an awareness of a vibration. It's the vibration of the atoms and cells of your body. You must learn to trust your feelings and become a believer in your own intuition and to recognize the times when your intuition is trying to make you aware of something.

Women are said to be more intuitive than men, who tend to get into their heads a bit too much and overanalyze. Of course, this is just a generalization; anyone can be intuitive, and anyone can be analytical. And don't think intuition is some bogus idea only for crystal rubbers and tree huggers. Intuition is a powerful tool in business. My first lesson in this was on the streets, where I had to have my "antennae" up all the time to avoid danger and capitalize on opportunity. My intuition saved my hide more times than I can count and kept me out of jail on more than one occasion. Because I had learned to trust my gut, it was natural for me to follow my hunch that real estate was the right career for me when that opportunity presented itself. And later, when my gut told me it was time to travel the world, I went. My intuition told me when to get into a major Internet deal in 1999, and it also told me when to get out, which was just before the market totally crashed. Had I not procrastinated on my exit, taking five months to evaluate my feelings, I would have made many more millions than I did. This is by no means a complaint; I just want to be entirely clear about how important it is to be in touch with what you feel. Every time I have trusted my intuition—*every single time*—I have been led to something great.

To tap into your intuition, start feeling with your gut more and with your head less. When you're in your head, you process the "feeling" based on all your beliefs and past conditioning and not on your higher self that just knows. Your intuition can be developed by paying attention, slowing down, and becoming aware of what's inside instead of outside yourself. The meditation practices offered in chapter 9 will be especially helpful for you.

## YOUR REAL POWER CENTER AND SOURCE: THE SUBCONSCIOUS AND ITS THREE FUNCTIONS

The subconscious is sometimes called the unconscious, spiritual self, higher self, and so on. The name is irrelevant. Choose one you like and get to know how it works. One of the goals in life is to really discover this godlike side of yourself. The more you do so, the more you can become and create with your life and individual talents.

Your subconscious, the part of your mind of which you are mostly unaware, is the booster I referred to earlier. If the power of the conscious part of you is life to the first degree, then the power of your subconscious is life to the millionth degree. It is absolutely amazing, yet few people even know how it works, let alone teach others to use it. Because it is metaphorically hidden from you most of the time, it receives little or no attention or explanation as you grow up, especially not in schools. It rarely gets any attention when you're an adult, either.

Let's change that!

**First and foremost, the subconscious keeps you alive and operates all of your vital bodily functions.** This includes the regeneration of your cells, which die and are replaced constantly. **It is a power source you cannot see, yet it is working absolute miracles with every breath you take.**

Your subconscious regulates your heart, digests your food, and keeps your body's temperature just perfect. It could take many chapters to cover all the unseen bodily functions your subconscious regulates—and it has; just consult medical texts or mind-body books to see for yourself. Suffice it to say you couldn't consciously keep track of everything it did every second to keep you alive.

> *Not everything that is faced can be changed, but nothing can be changed until it is faced.*
>
> *—James Baldwin*

**Second, the subconscious stores all the experiences, habits, and beliefs you have ever developed.** The subconscious automatically regulates every habit you have and makes absolutely certain that it runs the "program" without you having to worry about it. Your subconscious is your operating system. Modern computing seems like child's play compared to the power at your disposal.

Once a habit is fixed in your subconscious, it's on autopilot just like all the other programs you've created in your life. This system is a marvel to behold. **It can act as your greatest friend or devastate you if the wrong programs get started—because once they get going, they're not always easy to stop.** Consider some common habits, like fingernail biting or using the words *um* or *like* all the time. If you've ever tried to break yourself of one of these ingrained habits, you know how persistent they can be. I used to bite my nails as a kid, and so did my son Keenan, until we used some positive affirmations and visualization techniques to help him break the habit. (We also put spicy stuff on his nails, so when he did put them in his mouth, the results were definitely not to his taste.) It took three weeks of continuous effort, but he did it, and he's only seven. He had a couple of setbacks and we went right back to the program, and now he's not biting his nails anymore.

That should tell you that it takes serious *conscious* effort to rewire behaviors rooted in the subconscious, but it's not difficult. The same applies to every other habit you might have, positive or negative, from the way you tie your shoes to your beliefs about money to the way you work with other people.

The greatest challenge you face is that once a habit is fixed in the subconscious, you attract and are attracted to everything in alignment with it. (You'll learn more about how your habits and beliefs are created and changed in chapter 4.) This happens whether or not you like it, and whether or not you like the results. If, for example, your belief is that people can't be trusted, then you'll be drawn into friendships with people who hold the same belief, who are not trustworthy themselves, and who thereby support your belief. You might not even notice when honest people show up in your life, because honesty just isn't on your radar screen or part of the vibration you're in. While you could recognize honesty in someone else (you won't necessarily be blind to it, though you'll be suspicious), you won't be drawn to it unless and until you acknowledge the limitation and work on the subconscious to change the belief.

To see a permanent change on the outside, you must first create the change of belief on the inside. Failing to do so is the reason people who go on a diet frequently gain all the weight back. They use willpower to starve themselves but don't change the "program" and self-image that makes them eat what they do.

The subconscious does not have the ability to reject a command or habit that has been impressed on it. Think of what hypnotists do to willing participants. They bypass the conscious side of people's personalities, and through autosuggestion they get their subjects to bark like a dog or create a sour taste in their mouth, just by getting into the subconscious mind. The lesson? **The subcon-**

scious does not do the thinking. That is not its function. It just carries out orders. Think of it as your personal genie at your beck and call twenty-four hours a day, seven days a week, on duty when you are awake or asleep.

**The third part of your subconscious is the truly magical part.** It's the side of you that connects you on a nonphysical level with the entire Universal Intelligence and energy fields. There's no line separating these energy fields. There must be millions of different frequencies of energy, and with your subconscious mind you can tap right into the source of all the supply.

You know from physics that everything you see and cannot see is essentially energy, constantly in a state of motion and vibration. It's the energy and information you can't see that the subconscious can access. The intelligent energy in you is connected to all other energy fields and intelligence, and whatever you want to create in your life begins with desire and thought.

**Thoughts are just things in a different vibration.** It doesn't matter if it's a new body you want or more financial success; it all works the same way. Once you align your habits and beliefs with what you want, your subconscious moves your vibration immediately in harmony with whatever you need to create the physical equivalent of your thought. This is why you must choose your thoughts wisely. You get and become exactly what you think about most.

When you consciously choose the thoughts you need to be in the vibration you want, you start to impress these thoughts on your subconscious. Over time, a new and more powerful program is created and you have a permanent frequency set up, just like you can program your car radio's buttons for your favorite station. Once the "station" is selected, everything in the universe that is in harmony with it immediately starts to move into physical form.

As you think different thoughts, you cause your body to vibrate in harmony with whatever you are thinking. That's why it's so important to have positive thoughts. **Only positive thoughts attract positive, and negative thoughts attract negative.** Most people focus on exactly what they don't want and wonder why it always shows up: they tune in to WIDW ("What I Don't Want") and are surprised that's the station they hear. Remember you can choose the station, you can move the dial so the receiver tunes in the frequency you want.

Many people confuse the Universal Intelligence by not being clear enough about what they want or by constantly changing the image in their heads. They channel surf. To realize the results you want in life, you must "stay tuned."

The nonphysical part of the world is where all the real power is. It's like the nuclear power plant to which each of us has equal and total access: anytime, anywhere. Most people plug into the equivalent of wall sockets when they have the choice and ability to plug into the infinite source of *all* supply.

Through thought, you can tap into this great resource. Your job is to choose what you want to create, hold onto that image as clearly and as often as you can, and allow whatever it is you desire to move from the nonphysical to the physical. This does not mean that you just wait and see. You are responsible for doing everything you can to get closer to the goal you desire, as well.

## PLANT GOOD THOUGHTS

Regard your thoughts as seeds, no different from the tiny seed of a carrot, or an acorn from an oak tree. When the gardener plants a seed, the first duty is accomplished. The second duty is to take care of the seed by watering it and ensuring that what needs to happen under the surface can happen. You don't dig up a seed on a daily basis to see whether or not it has grown. You trust that it will. You know this because humans have been planting simple seeds for thousands of years, and most of them sprout under the right conditions.

There's the challenge: Most people are so grounded in their physicality that they want instant gratification, and they lose their patience if they cannot see results immediately. They want proof because without proof nothing is happening . . . so they think. But everything worth creating is worth the joy of watching it unfold.

I have watched in awe the creation and development of amazing things in my life, most notably my two sons. I have, by contrast, also watched the destruction of people's lives because of their choices and lack of understanding. Therefore, I have always said that ignorance is not bliss; it is a shame.

The truth is that you don't know how many days, weeks, or years it takes to create something from the nonphysical universe into the physical. I suggest that you believe without the physical evidence, holding onto the truth that the universe is perfect and will move into form whatever you desire if you just do the planting and take care of the seeds. Have faith.

### CHAPTER 3

# The Great Law and The Seven Natural Laws That Will Change Your Life Forever

*Nothing puzzles me more than time and space, and yet nothing troubles me less.*

*—Charles Lamb*

The universe operates perfectly. It's mind-boggling when you think of everything that happens around you and inside you that you take for granted. Think about the oceans, the planets, nature, the gallons of blood pulsing through your veins and arteries. Each is a piece of perfection operating by precise laws.

When you learn how you fit and function in this precision, it's much easier to appreciate who you really are and how you can create a wholly successful life. **It's time to celebrate your inherent greatness and to understand you were created perfectly.** It's time to stop limiting your abilities with your insecurities and inaccurate beliefs.

Each one of the laws in this chapter relates directly to your everyday life. It is not an accident that these laws exist, and no matter what your belief is regarding who or what created them, the laws are irrefutable. Understanding these laws and how you can use and coexist with them will forever change your life.

The primary impact on me has been to create a sense of discernment and even detachment from circumstances. As soon as I judge something, I now recognize that I am introducing my ego into the equation, as well as my beliefs. Whenever any situation arises and I can think of it in the context of the laws you are about to learn, instead of jumping to mental or emotional conclusions, I experience a calmness in knowing everything is turning out the way it should be.

Knowing these laws has kept me calm when business deals didn't turn out as I had hoped. You will read in this chapter about a time when I walked away from a partnership and three hundred thousand dollars of my own money with grace and generosity, which ended up leading me to make millions just three years later. At the time, I could have been upset or angry, but I wasn't because I knew it would work out if I really believed one thing: **Everything happens exactly the way it is supposed to, and some things just aren't to my personal taste.** Getting divorced was hard emotionally, but what got me through was trusting that the universe was simply operating precisely as it should. Seeing my two sons as a result of one of those marriages is to see the perfection in the creative forces. If I knew then what it would be like to have my two guys now, I would have peeled the skin off my bones for the joy I get today. However, during the pain, it's hard to see what good might come years later. Understanding the laws you'll learn in this chapter, I've learned to roll with the rhythm of life and to accept whatever I attract, including hardship.

Once you understand these laws as I do and understand that everything is connected, they'll take on a new meaning. They are like an exact map to follow. Once you read and think about each of the laws, reflect on how you can apply it to your past experiences. Of course, in creating a masterpiece of the now and potential future, you should give each law even more, deeper consideration. Take the time to consider and work in concert with these laws in your daily life and every action, and you'll experience both joy and calm in every area of your life.

## THE GREAT LAW
### *Energy is.*

Each of the seven natural laws is a corollary to one great, over-arching law: *Everything is energy.* In other words, we live in a kind of energy soup. Every molecule that makes up every bit of matter contains a huge amount of energy. Energy, which is essentially dimensionless, is everywhere and in everything. Quantum mechanics tells us that even a vacuum, which most of us believe contains nothing, has energy. In fact, Dr. William Tiller, professor emeritus at Stanford University, tells us that *just one hydrogen atom* contains about one trillion times more energy than what is contained in all the physical mass of all the planets, plus all the stars in our universe, out to a radius of twenty billion light-years. **Clearly, energy is not about space. After all, the hydrogen atom is tiny and our universe is vast. Energy is about potential.**

Ultimately, every one of us, our planet, and the universe in which it resides are made of, emit, and receive energy.

We have light energy, heat energy, sound energy, magnetic energy, thought energy, kinetic energy, atomic energy, mechanical energy, and so on. There are millions of levels of frequencies, all interconnected. We also have electromagnetic, gamma, and radio, just to really make the point. X-rays are a type of energy that can penetrate solids, as can gamma rays, due to their rate of vibration. In the end, they are just forms of what everything, including us, is made of: energy. The seven corollaries below tell us how all kinds of energy operate in the natural world, in our everyday lives.

## 1. THE LAW OF VIBRATION AND ATTRACTION
### *Everything in our universe constantly vibrates and moves.*

Both the nonphysical and the physical aspects of our universe are made up of energy and intelligence that vibrates or, in other words, oscillates, resonates, pulsates. Nothing rests. The difference between the physical and nonphysical is the rate of vibration. This law is responsible for the difference between what we can see with our naked eye, like our hands, for example, and that which we cannot see but is there, like a radio wave.

A table appears to be solid and stationary; however, if you looked through a powerful microscope, you would actually see movement with lots of space between the molecules. With the help of a microscope, you are able to perceive the slowest vibratory rate of the table's molecules. The same is true with your body. As I've mentioned before, although your body looks the same from day to day, *it isn't the same body.* You are shedding millions of cells all the time and replacing them with new ones. Even though you cannot see it happening, it is.

> *We are what we repeatedly do. Excellence, then, is not an act, but a habit.*
> —Aristotle

Thoughts and feelings are also energy. Whenever you are sensitive to someone else's feelings, whenever you become aware of your own feelings, this is conscious perception of a vibration. Whenever you say, "I feel good," or "I feel bad," you are commenting on whether your vibration is positive or negative in your own mind. You can also decide to feel good or bad (vibrations) by choosing your thoughts. As we've already established, only you can choose your thoughts, and you decide when and even the kind of thought energy to send and receive. If you choose negative thoughts, you emit a "negative" vibration or frequency and therefore align yourself with that frequency. On the other hand, when you choose positive thoughts, you do the exact opposite and tune into and attract the "positive" frequency of intelligence and energy. Whether vibrations are good or bad depends on you; it is totally based on your own interpretation, and your brain is the instrument you use to move your entire being into the vibration you choose. It is your vibratory switching station.

Your brain is the most powerful electromagnetic processing tool ever created, and if you use it wisely to choose positive thoughts, everything you desire will start to move your way until it materializes in its physical counterpart. The more you focus and concentrate, the faster and more potent the frequency gets. This is no different from using a magnifying glass outside to start a fire using the sun's energy. (We'll explore the power of focus in chapter 8.)

**Another way of stating this law is "like attracts like," meaning that people will attract energies like them.** In relationships, this means people who are similar to each other (especially those who share the same or complementary beliefs) tend to be attracted to one another. It happens in business, romance, and social circles.

My experience with Bamboo.com was probably one of the most powerful examples of attraction I have seen in my life. This fabulous company was built around the then-new technology of virtual touring, the ability to conceptually view video on the Internet to allow people to see and vicariously experience a location without having to go there. Bamboo staked its claim in the real estate niche, completely capturing that market segment. I was fortunate to be asked to play on this cutting-edge team just as the technology was first taking hold.

The opportunity to be Bamboo's sales and marketing strategist came to me by way of Len McCurdy, a man I'd met a few years earlier just as I was leaving a business partnership. Len was mediating the dissolution of our company, and he told me at the time that he was impressed with the way I handled myself during the proceedings: gently, firmly, generously, I walked away from a business that no longer fit with my goals, leaving more than three hundred thousand dollars of my own money in the business. So when Len was looking for someone for his son's start-up, he thought of me as a person who would match and complement their style of business management.

He was right. In addition to being electric with creativity, this new company was also a lovefest, constantly attracting and keeping some of the best minds with whom I've ever had the privilege to work. We hired people with phenomenal potential and helped them believe in themselves and the mission we were a part of. Our marketing and sales departments were built on personal development, not sales skills. Essentially, we taught them everything you're learning in this book, and we developed a team mind-set of "We can do anything individually and more together." As a result, it was an amazing team: We acquired a hundred thousand customers in just nine months, producing sales of many millions per month.

We called ourselves the Four-Minute Mile Team, after the

legendary, record-breaking run of Roger Bannister, wherein he was the first man ever to finish the mile in under four minutes; remarkably, as soon as he'd done it, other athletes were able to do it, too—simply because now they knew it could be done. We were dedicated to doing what seemed impossible, to breaking our own records. We gave our people the training they needed, and then we put them to the test. As long as they could run that four-minute mile, figuratively of course, they were on the team. That kind of energy attracts more like it, so many of the people who were employed by Bamboo came there because they were friends with someone already working with us. It seemed everyone wanted to be part of that energy and creative force.

When the company merged with Ipix in 2000, the corporate culture changed drastically and it was no longer the right environment for me. Although it was hard to say good-bye to many of the people I'd brought onboard there, it was time to move on. My intuition told me so.

Logically, if like attracts like, unlike repels unlike, too. (You'll read more about this in the next section on the law of polarity.) This was what moved me to leave Bamboo, and I'd already seen this at work when my marriages ended. But until I met my girl-friend Maria, I had paid no real attention to the law of attraction in romantic relationships. Kind of crazy, huh? Not to consider attraction in the context of romance? That's not to say I had never been attracted to someone before; of course I had been. Attracted enough to get married twice! But that's not the same thing as working in concert with the law of attraction. After I divorced for the second time, I realized I needed to improve my relationship radar. In addition to learning from the mistakes I had made before—especially getting married too quickly, for reasons other than deep, passionate love, as well as neglecting honest communication, particularly not telling my partners my true feelings—I decided to put the law of attraction to work for me.

Imagining in detail my ideal romantic partner, I wrote it all down on a piece of paper and tucked it away for safekeeping. I had poured out my heart, my desire to meet and love a person who wanted to have fun with me, was attractive and spontaneous, would be family-centered, and so on, including details about our emotional and physical intimacy.

I then decided to take things slowly with whomever I dated, meaning we'd keep things casual and be upfront about it. I figured that I had put in my order with the universe, and if the right woman showed up, I'd know it, but there was no reason to rush things, either.

Maria and I met at our gym, and as we did with everyone else, we dated casually. We had a great time together and got to know one another. For the first three years of our relationship, we made no commitments beyond enjoying one another's company. And then we decided to make ours a monogamous relationship. It wasn't long before I showed Maria the description I'd written of my ideal woman. I had described her to a tee, and it was hard for her to believe how precisely the details fit her. As for me, I couldn't stop grinning: Here was the woman I had wanted right before my eyes, and here was attraction operating precisely according to its law.

It's a cliché that birds of a feather flock together, and this is just one more way of describing the law of vibration and attraction. I once heard from financial author Robert Allen that your income will be the average of your ten closest friends' incomes—again, your surroundings reflect your own perception of reality. Is this true for you? Think of your friends, the vacations you take, the places where you dine. You meet people who are like you. Think of your work: Who has been attracted to the same company? Why do you think they have been attracted there? Look at the leader of that firm, and you'll see traces of that person in each employee—not exact matches but traces. *Entrepreneurs and business owners take note:* If you don't like what you see among your personnel, you know where to look first for clues about what should change—maybe it's a part of you.

## 2. THE LAW OF POLARITY
### *Everything in the universe has an equal and exact opposite.*

In Eastern philosophy, the law of polarity is referred to as yin and yang. It is one of the simpler laws to understand: If something is hot, for example, then there exists a polar opposite that must be, by law, equally cold. Here in the West, we say, "Every cloud has a silver lining."

Success in life can be greatly enhanced by always remembering this law whenever we face a huge challenge. Our initial perception may be that the circumstances are negative, but according to this law, there must be an equally positive opportunity inherent in the challenge. The quicker we learn to look for the opportunities, the quicker the negative disappears from our perception, and the quicker our energy changes. Even some of our most painful life experiences can be shown to have a positive side. I know my two divorces were incredibly difficult times in my life, but they also yielded powerful self-examination and growth. Which reminds me of a slightly naughty joke that I can't resist telling you:

*Why is divorce so expensive?*

*Because it's worth it.*

That's funny because it's true—the financial and emotional pain of divorce has its flip side, usually freedom of some kind, which in retrospect almost always feels more important than those temporary pains. We simply have to remember that it's only our *perception* that causes us to believe something is good or bad, since both are present in everything. Our perceptions create what we deem "reality," yet there's no such thing as an absolute reality. The only reality is our own.

Recognizing the fluid nature of reality and the natural opposition in every situation is a vital skill, yet it takes practice. Your job is to get past your tendency to hastily judge and label everything and understand that everything has an up and a down, a good and a bad, an inside and an outside. This applies to your emotions, your physical body, your relationships, and all else. Learn to see both sides of each and every situation and your life will flow much smoother and results will begin to appear.

Everyone with whom I discuss this law asks about how it applies to extreme cases, such as a child's illness, or a loved one's death, or acts of war. My only response is that I have one hundred percent belief in God and the infinite intelligence of the *whole universe.* I agree that those occurrences encompass the worst of human suffering; it still does not change where you are, and who you are, or that you must find peace and love in your heart and have total faith always. Once your physical body is gone, your essence, your spirit, becomes ever more a part of that which created you. Your physical illusion of being separate disappears. If you have death of one thing, you must by law have life somewhere else.

Can you see how some of the most difficult circumstances in your own life, either in the past or right now, have the seed of opportunity? Can you also see how recognizing and embracing the positive in every situation moves you in the direction of your dreams? And how refusing to do so will work against you? In fact, refusing works against you on two levels: If you don't accept both the good along with the bad in life, you are also resisting the next law, the law of rhythm.

## 3. THE LAW OF RHYTHM
### Everything is moving in perfect rhythm and at perfect speed.

The tide flows in, and the tide ebbs out. If you stand at the shore, rigid and unwilling to go with the flow, the surf can crash over you and even knock you down. But if you're willing to bend, to relax, to enjoy the swells, you can actually catch a nice wave every now and then.

Have you ever been caught in an undertow? If you have and didn't know how currents work, you probably used up so much energy fighting it that you were exhausted. The best way to get out of the current is to just swim across it instead of against it. It doesn't matter how strong a swimmer you are—fighting is futile.

I learned this lesson at the Copa Cabana beach in Rio de Janeiro. I had been a competitive swimmer

> Your life and my life flow into each other as wave flows into wave, and unless there is peace and joy and freedom for you, there can be no real peace or joy or freedom for me. To see reality—not as we expect it to be, but as it is—is to see that unless we live for each other and in and through each other, we do not really live very satisfactorily; that there can really be life only where there really is, in just this sense, love.
>
> —Fredrick Buechner

in my youth and a triathlete as an adult, so when I visited there in my twenties, I thought I was safe in the ocean, although I'd trained only in lakes and swimming pools. Then I found myself caught in a major current one day. I thought I would just outswim it, go against it, and make my way back to shore. Wrong! Here I was, this strapping young guy, trying to battle the ocean and losing. I nearly died that day.

What I didn't realize was that if I had swum across the current, I'd have gotten out of it. Or if I had just let it carry me, within about a hundred yards I'd have been out of it. With some luck and lot of stamina, I finally made it out of the water, exhausted and having learned a profound lesson about the nature of currents and my will to live.

Not fighting feels totally unnatural to the person who isn't familiar with how currents work, but the universe is fairly relentless. If you simply don't know a law and break it, you don't get cut a lot of slack, kind of like making a right-hand turn on a red light in a state where it's illegal. Just because you're from out of state and thought it was okay to turn on the red light doesn't mean a cop won't pull you over and be completely justified in citing you with a moving violation.

Back to my point: The ocean has a great deal to teach you about the rhythms of life. You must recognize when you're in a current and when you're resisting the natural rhythm, whether it's in your personal or business life. There's a rhythm that occurs at all times.

Think about how relationships can feel in and out of sync. How is it that one minute you can feel so lovey-dovey, and the next you're ready to jump off a bridge? The same is true with your job. At one moment you can be completely ecstatic, and the next minute a phone call comes in to tell you a deal just went south.

You cannot force the good times to continue always, nor can you force anything in life to happen. The planets orbit in perfect rhythm, and so do you. Life has seasons, both figuratively and literally. Some are longer than others, and some are harsher than others.

There are times when things seem out of rhythm—or are simply in a rhythm that makes you uncomfortable. Your job is to stay focused on your vision and go with the flow instead of resisting it. Most people waste too much time and energy resisting, yet no one can change the seasons. You can choose whether to stay warm in winter or gripe about the cold. Better yet, you can decide to learn to ski.

> *Love is what we are born with. Fear is what we learn. The spiritual journey is the unlearning of fear and prejudices and the acceptance of love back into our hearts. Love is the essential reality and our purpose on earth. To be consciously aware of it, to experience love in ourselves and others, is the meaning of life. Meaning does not lie in things. Meaning lies in us.*
> —Marianne Williamson

## 4. THE LAW OF RELATIVITY
### *Everything is relative.*

Are you short or tall? Is this book heavy or light? Is the room you're in big or small? Do you earn a lot of money or a little bit? My point is that until you relate or compare the thing in question to something else, you cannot answer. You actually cannot define something without having something to relate to it, something for comparison.

Another way of saying this is that what may be good for one person may not be good for another. A fifteen-hundred-square-foot home may be small for someone accustomed to living in a bigger house, but it could feel like a palace to someone else who's never lived in a house at all. Your past experiences influence your evaluations, but the truth is that everything just is. A fifteen-hundred-square-foot home is not *actually* small or large. It's just a fifteen-hundred-square-foot home, perceived and described by different people as being cozy, claustrophobic, or enormous, depending upon their perspectives.

It is useful to keep this law in mind when you are evaluating a situation or event. It can get you in trouble if you keep seeing something that someone has or can do as "more" than what you have or can do. Everything is relative, and you must learn not to compare to others or to past experiences. Look at things as "just is" without judgment, and you'll never succumb to feeling like you're not enough or that you don't have enough.

## 5. THE LAW OF CAUSE AND EFFECT
*For every cause there is an effect, and for every effect there is a cause.*

For every action we take, there is an effect. If you send good thoughts out, good comes back. If you give love, love comes back. If you give away money, money flows back to you. According to physics, there is an equal and opposite reaction for every action. According to this natural law, whatever you send out or give comes right back in the same or different energy form. Good karma, as some call it, leads to good karma. Of course, the opposite is true, too.

Some people have a hard time remembering that this applies to money just as much as anything else. After all, money is just an idea. We created the green paper with ink on it to represent money. Money is energy just like everything else. There are laws governing what you must do to acquire money, which are no different from a farmer having to plant seeds before he harvests; e.g., you simply cannot get and keep something greater than you have given. You must be more and give more to have more.

I teach this law to my children by encouraging them to be "go-givers" instead of go-getters. This Thanksgiving, for example, after a big family dinner, all the kids bolted to go and play. Keenan and Noah, however, stayed to help clear the tables. I requested each of them help ten people and take their dishes to the kitchen. So off they went, and when they were done, they both came back to me beaming! Someone had given each of them a dollar for their efforts. They hadn't expected it, but they got it. Every week they earn two dollars allowance, so fifteen minutes of helping really paid off for them. Incidentally, their "financial plan" allows them to put seventy-five cents in the bank each week, spend seventy-five cents, and donate fifty cents. Not a bad ratio for most adults to emulate.

## 6. THE LAW OF GENDER
### *Both male and female are necessary for creation.*

Think of the give and take in conversation. It is the perfect illustration of the law of gender in a seemingly genderless context: One person speaks, asserting an idea or giving instruction or posing a question; the other person listens, receiving the communication. Then, ideally, roles reverse and the person who had been speaking listens and the person who had been listening speaks. Out of this exchange, new ideas emerge, new plans are made, new agreements are formed. These two complementary energies— giving and taking—give rise to a new creation.

The law of gender manifests in all living things as masculine and feminine. In our example, speaking is the masculine energy (asserting), and listening is the female energy (receiving). You may have already recognized that the law of gender is closely allied with the law of polarity; it's another facet of the yin-yang principle.

This law governs creation, yet the word *creation* is often erroneously used, for nothing is ever really created. All new things merely result from the changing of something that was into something that now is. The law of gender manifests in the animal kingdom as sex, male and female counterparts within species. It also manifests in the mineral and vegetable kingdoms. Without the dual principle of male and female there could not be a difference of potential, perpetuation of motion, nor regeneration.

This law is also referred to as the creative law. It decrees that everything in nature is both male and female. Both are required for life to come into existence. This law also decrees that all seeds, including and especially thought seeds, have a gestation or incubation period before they manifest. This is why it's imperative to allow the appropriate time to pass for a thought or image to move into its physical counterpart.

## 7. THE LAW OF PERPETUAL TRANSMUTATION OF ENERGY
*Energy is forever moving into and out of different forms.*

This last law is a mouthful, but learning exactly what it is and how it works is imperative to creating whatever you desire.

As you now know, according to the great law and its first corollary, the law of vibration and attraction, the entire universe is made up of energy, and all of it is moving at varying rates of speed. All energy fields are connected. From the physical body that you and I can touch, see, and feel, to the sun's rays, all are connected. Therefore, we have this last corollary, the seventh natural law: All energy is constantly flowing from one form or vibration into another form or vibration. It also moves from a higher plane (the nonphysical) to a lower plane (the physical).

Think about this example. The sun's rays (heat, light, and electromagnetic energy) shine on a tomato plant, which uses the sun's energy to grow by making molecules. Energy is stored in the plant molecules, and that energy is passed to you when you eat the tomato and convert the plant's energy into what you need for your own activities. You can use that energy, now called *metabolic* energy, to ride a bicycle up a hill, using mechanical energy to pedal, converting that energy to *kinetic* (movement) energy. At the top of the hill, kinetic energy has put you in a position to roll down the other side, which means you now have potential energy. When you go down the hill, *potential* energy becomes kinetic, causing the bike to roll down the hill seemingly of its own volition. This is just one sequence of events that shows the transmutation of energy through many forms. A simpler example is this. When I rub my hands together, I am using metabolic energy that is stored in my cells from a tomato (or some other energy-rich plant or animal). As I rub my hands, I am actually creating heat, which is then released back into the atmosphere, and the cycle goes on and on as before.

Perpetual transmutation just means that energy is constantly and forever moving into and out of different forms, never created or destroyed. Some energy you can see; some you cannot. As a matter of fact, most you cannot see with your eyes. Different forms of energy are penetrating your every molecule with every breath you take. Keep in mind that this natural law says that *nothing* is constant. Everything is forever moving into and out of form.

The beauty of this law is that your thoughts are considered the most potent form of energy that penetrates all space and time. They have the inherent potential to transmute from the nonphysical to the physical *all the time*.

### CHAPTER 4

# The Importance of Your Beliefs and Self-Esteem

*The greatest discovery of my generation is that human beings can alter their lives by altering their attitudes of mind.*

*—William James*

My experiences in the gang gave me many beliefs I had to overcome to rebuild my self-esteem; that you already know. But you might be surprised to hear that there were also some beliefs I adopted on the streets that later were of major help to me in my legitimate professional life. For example, because I had spent most of my years as the orchestrator rather than the implementer of our activities, I thought of myself as being good at organizing the right activities to achieve an outcome. I had worked out the logistics, deployed the right amount of people to do each job, maintained records of our transactions, and been successful in keeping most of us out of trouble with the law. So I thought of myself as being an excellent planner, a big-picture thinker, an idea man, a talented manager, all of which came in handy both in my position as CEO with RE/MAX in Indiana and later as senior vice president in charge of Bamboo's sales and marketing. The streets taught me to trust my gut, to take risks, to negotiate, and to reinvest in my business.

You have thousands of beliefs, both positive and negative, that cause you to perceive and act a certain way. The effects of your beliefs are not as abstract as you might think. Let's say you're looking at a restaurant menu. You'll make a decision and take action by ordering and eating the food that aligns with your beliefs about health and nutrition. The result of that decision will determine whether or not you'll have an abundance of energy. It will determine, over a period of time, your external appearance. It will also determine your internal health. As you can see, one small decision affects a whole range of things. Choosing improperly for long periods is a surefire route to a mediocre life.

What you must consider is whether or not your beliefs can get you to the destination of your dreams. Perhaps you've heard about how elephants are trained to stand tied to a tiny stake in the ground, which they could easily pull up simply by using their considerable strength against the restraint. When an elephant is young, the trainer uses a heavy chain with a shackle around the calf's ankle, which causes painful sores. Within a short period of time, the animal is conditioned that pulling equals pain. As the elephant matures, the trainer can use a weaker and weaker tether because the elephant won't test it, until a simple rope tied to a tent stake will keep this five-ton animal from roaming. It's likely that many of the beliefs you have today are acting like that weak rope, perhaps holding you in place and preventing you from going where you want to be. That's why people stay in relationships that aren't working, keep a job they don't like, continue neglecting their health, and so on. The good news is you can change. You can break free. You can *choose* your beliefs.

Most people come to this realization about religion at some point in life: You don't have to attend the same church as your parents did, you don't have to teach your children the same creed, and you don't have to believe in the same deity. If you've ever faced this in your life, you realize both how liberating and powerful a choice this is. It can also be frightening, a little like flying without a net. How can you know what's "right" if you aren't basing it on what someone else has taught you? This kind of choice requires you to truly listen to yourself, consult your own wisdom, and assess your own private spirituality. Whether you chose to continue the tradition of your family in your faith, or you chose to go another way, you probably felt a sense of maturity and responsibility in *your choice*. That's because it was your choice, which has more meaning and personal commitment than if someone else makes the decision for you.

Likewise, when a marriage is tested, and both partners decide to stay in the marriage, they can come to a powerful realization: *Every day, every minute, every second together is a choice.* Their commitment becomes deeper and more meaningful when both partners are *consciously* choosing one another all the time instead of just going along with the program, not thinking about the fact that they don't have to be married. Choosing one another with this awareness is a far greater act of love and adds richness to the relationship.

It can be the same with all of your beliefs. **Consciously choosing what to believe, whether it's about health, God, marriage, children, career, other people, or anything else gives those beliefs more weight, more meaning in your life.** I chose to hold onto some of the beliefs I adopted on the street—being a risk-taker, trusting my instincts, believing in myself as a manager and even a visionary—

and, of course, I decided to jettison those beliefs that were holding me back. Thinking I was not smart enough, that people didn't like me, and that I couldn't trust anyone else were definitely not going to get me where I wanted to go. I realized, through the help of many mentors, that for anything in my life to change, I had to change. It works from the inside out, not from the outside in.

It's not exactly like flipping a switch, though. It takes some time if you've been living as if these beliefs are true with a capital T; in other words, if you've become so attached to your beliefs that they seem absolute, as if they are not just your beliefs but as if your life depended on them. Once a belief is anchored in the psyche, all actions will just be automatic and in accordance with what you believe, nothing less and nothing more.

We tend to identify so strongly with our beliefs that admitting one needs to change is like saying, "I am not enough the way I am." Well, guess what? **In the same way that you are not your body, you are not your beliefs.** And in some areas of your life, your beliefs may not be enough to get you the result you want.

> *While it is true that without a vision the people perish, it is doubly true that without action the people and their vision perish, as well.*
> *—Johnetta Betsch Cole*

Ask yourself whether your most dearly held beliefs are serving you or not. Do they help you create the life of your dreams? Or do they limit you and the people you love? Remember that beliefs are like blinders for humans. They can be so powerful that they cause you to see only what's in line with them. Yet they are not the truth. They are just your perception of the truth, based on your past teachings, experiences, and evaluations.

## WHERE BELIEFS ARE BORN

Your beliefs are fostered from birth by your parents, teachers, other kids, the evaluations your make about experiences, and the meaning you associate with that experience. Reading, writing, self-talk, and watching television also influence your beliefs, which in turn create and created all your habits that are now mostly on autopilot and are run by your subconscious.

You have beliefs about what kind of person you are intellectually, morally, and spiritually. You have beliefs as to whether or not you are a good provider, whether or not you are a good lover or dancer. You have literally thousands of self-images in various areas of your life. All of them are illusions based merely on belief, yet they feel so real. Your self-image is what you at the deepest level believe to be true about yourself. After all, you've gotten enough proof over the years, haven't you? It takes some serious reprogramming to combat all that "evidence."

Don't get caught between who you really are and some of the results you've been getting. Be bold enough and smart enough to see past where you are right now and take hold of what's rightfully yours.

Two people can have the exact same experience, such as going really fast down a roller coaster. One loves it and the other is petrified. Do you think that one person may end up with a belief that roller coasters are scary while the person next to him ends up with a belief that roller coasters are exhilarating? You bet. Different people form absolute opposite beliefs about all kinds of experiences all the time. Which beliefs are true? Neither. Or both. But the real question is which beliefs will get you where you want to go in life. *You get to choose.*

I'll give you another example from my own life that happened when my son, Keenan, was seven. I was invited to go paragliding in San Diego and accepted. Keenan said he'd love to go as well, so I called his mom and left her a message inviting her to join us at the glider port at 11:30 A.M., when we would jump off a cliff harnessed to an instructor.

Well, I am definitely the adventurous one, and she is not.

She hurried to the glider port to watch and almost fainted as our son ran off the cliff harnessed to the instructor. The ocean was just five hundred feet below. Some of the spectators couldn't believe that I allowed my son to do this; others wished their kids were there to do it, too. It was the first time paragliding for both my son and me, so I didn't know what to expect. And yes, I was a little scared, but not as scared as when I'd gone skydiving. Five hundred feet seemed like a walk in the park compared to jumping from ten thousand feet up, where people look as small as ants.

My son's initial belief was, "WOW! This will be so much fun!" After the experience, his positive belief and perception about heights and paragliding were forever ingrained in his mind. His mom's first thought was that this would be dangerous. Her negative belief was slightly rattled by our experience, and she has even expressed a desire, although small, to maybe try it herself sometime. I hope she does.

By the way, my five-and-a-half-year-old son, Noah, was not ready to go that day, so I just let him know that it was his decision and I respected that. After his brother got back, beaming from one ear to the other, and he saw the photos that we had taken from the air, Noah said that maybe he'd go next time, too.

Some beliefs are formed instantly, such as when a significant emotional experience occurs, like paragliding for my son, and other beliefs are formed over time or after several experiences. What's important to remember is that beliefs aren't good or bad; they just *are*. The key is to understand the ones you have and determine whether or not they're serving you and helping you create the life you really want.

## USE WRITING, VISUALIZATION, AND MEDITATION TO STAY ON COURSE

When a plane leaves any airport, even after the pilot puts in the coordinates of the final destination, the flight path must be continuously monitored and adjusted to keep the plane on course. Due to winds, weather, or other conditions, the plane will normally and constantly stray from the flight plan. Then it's up to the pilot to bring it back on course. That's why knowing the final destination is so critical.

Likewise, once you make up your mind to create the life of your dreams, it's up to you to stay on course despite the conditions. Your beliefs about how you handle adversity and challenges will determine what you do in times of stress and turbulence.

The most important point to remember is that your self-image and your beliefs are not fixed. **You can change your self-image and beliefs whenever you choose.** We had no choice about the beliefs that were instilled in us by teachers, parents, and so on—they just gave us their best—but now that we're adults, we can *choose* the beliefs that will move us in the direction of our dreams.

If you were a computer programmer and the program you created wasn't doing what you wanted it to do, what would you do? You'd change it, wouldn't you? Your programs should be no different. The key for you is to continuously evaluate your results, which tell you what the program is doing. Some of your pro-gramming was good for you when you were a kid or when you were in another job, but not necessarily the right thing for you if you seek to grow and have more than you currently do.

There are innumerable ways to change your programming, from psychotherapy to neuro-linguistic programming to a whole host of other complicated-sounding techniques. I offer you one simple method that applies the same principle these more sophisticated reprogramming procedures do: Bombard your subconscious.

A long time ago, I learned to use writing as a powerful tool for change. I started by identifying a belief I wanted to change, and you'll get help with this for yourself in the next few chapters. You'll remember that one belief for me was that I wasn't smart enough. The beliefs I wanted to adopt were these: *I am a very intelligent person. My ability to learn and grow is excellent. I have all the tools I need to get anything done effectively and efficiently.* So I wrote those beliefs repeatedly, perhaps twenty times a day for about two weeks, and reread what I'd written several times a day. In a way, this writing is an "instruction" to the subconscious. It's not that you're trying to convince your conscious mind; instead, you're simply sending new information to the subconscious. **Through repetition and emotional conviction, you impress a new belief onto your subconscious to align your every cell with this new belief.** Behavior and attraction can then occur automatically.

Another way to create this repetition is by making a tape of yourself talking about your new belief, then listening to that tape every day, ideally twice or more a day. This tape method is effec-tive for all kinds of beliefs on subjects ranging from health to wealth, from business success to charitable contribution, from relationships to spirituality, from productivity to creativity. Your main time investment will be up front in making the tape, which can be as simple (just your recorded voice) or as elaborate (including music, sound effects, and so on), as short (just five minutes) or as long as you like. After your tape is complete, you can listen to it while driving, as you go to sleep, as you wake up in the morning. Be creative!

For example, if you want to adopt new beliefs about your health, a tape you prepare for yourself would be a great soundtrack for your workouts. To write the script, imagine what your life will be like as a result of adopting a new belief, and describe it all in the present tense. Incidentally, that's the only rule for this method: **Describe everything as if it's already happening.** A script to be used while running might start like this:

> I love how it feels to run because my body is in such great condition. I can feel my heart working, and my breath is strong and even. My quadriceps and calves are tested but don't burn out. I am a healthy, vibrant person who respects the body as the amazing vessel it is: home to my soul. I am in the zone and running better than I ever have before. I am getting faster and stronger every day . . .

As you reprogram yourself and listen to your audiotape, you can also add visualization, which is a key component of success in any endeavor. Top athletes visualize religiously, because they know it unlocks potential at a level that analysis and even physical practice don't reach. By repeatedly visualizing the outcome you want, you create new cells of recognition in your subconscious. This way, your body gets used to that behavior and then expects it. To use your audiotape to help you visualize, instead of just listening passively to the recording, close your eyes and picture everything happening exactly as you hear yourself describe it. (Not a good idea while running or driving, but you can do this at other times.) It's as if you've created a "movie" you can play over and over in your mind.

Of course, you don't necessarily need a tape to visualize. Visualization is simply the creation of a new idea or belief, where you paint a new scenario, adding color and imagining sound, smell, and so on. An entrepreneur might "see" the bustling office, the enthusiastic staff, envelopes being opened with checks for large amounts of money, the product going out to clients or customers in flawless fashion. You can also add some more advanced techniques by visualizing the old behavior or belief and then mentally covering it with the new. Author and personal development expert Anthony Robbins calls this a "swoosh" pattern. You say to yourself, "Whoosh!" as you mentally use the new pattern to whisk away the old one.

Some people are a little intimidated by visualization, which is one reason an audiotape can be helpful. But visualization doesn't have to be daunting. Try this for a minute. Close your eyes and think of yourself at a picnic on a breezy but warm spring day. (Okay, I realize you can't close your eyes and read at the same time, so just stop for a moment, close your eyes and get that picture in your mind . . .)

What happened? Could you practically hear the birds singing, smell the fresh-cut grass, and feel the soft breeze and sun's warmth on your face? Were you actually there? No, but when you visualize, you bypass the part of you that thinks (your conscious mind) and you get right into the part of you, the subconscious, that can do only as it is programmed or told by the conscious to do. It does not know the difference between a true event and one that is played out in your mind. Consider the many times when you are sleeping that you kick or jump or fly. You can do this in your dreams because you are in the realm of the subconscious where everything is possible and all that's required is that you want to do something—and you can do it.

When you're trying to change your own programming and giving new instructions to the subconscious, use as many ways to reinforce the new belief as possible. If you know of other tools that have worked for you in the past, use them. If not, use what you've learned here and what you'll learn in chapter 9 on meditation, too.

How often and how much? It's individual for every person, but my experience tells me the more impressions you subject the old program to, the faster you see results. **If you can visualize or meditate several times a day, do it.** I also suggest that you focus on only one or two major new beliefs at a time, and really work on those until you feel they're ingrained. If you choose just two every month or so, in a year you'll have installed up to *twenty-four new beliefs*. That will be life-changing!

Where should you begin? The next chapter will help you decide. In it, you'll discern your "true north," evaluate the results you've been getting until now, and identify the underlying beliefs that have produced these results, and in chapter 6 you'll determine what you need to believe to propel you forward to the life of your dreams.

**PART II**

# The Life Design Matrix

### CHAPTER 5

# Find Your True North

*I'm not a teacher, only a fellow-traveler of whom you asked the way. I pointed ahead—ahead of myself as well as you.*
—*George Bernard Shaw*

A s you read and work through this chapter, please be as honest and open with yourself as you have ever been, perhaps even more so. You're going to look closely at where your *past* thought processes, beliefs, and decisions have gotten you. It is critical for you to understand that the life you are now living is one hundred percent your doing. You have made the decisions, regardless of the circumstances, to get you to where you are today. It is imperative that you accept total responsibility for the results in your adult life. Regardless of what your parents, friends, husband, wife, teacher, girlfriend, or whomever have done or said, you always had a choice about how you reacted or acted. If the beliefs you learned from your teachers, parents, or anyone else are not the ones you want or need anymore, it's your responsibility to change them.

In the next few chapters, you'll be learning a system I call the Life Design Matrix. **When you combine all the elements, you'll end up with a detailed and well-thought-out system for** *having it all:*

**a brief overview of your life as you want it to be and a daily plan of action, including targeting two beliefs and two goals for your attention.** This will come out of an in-depth assessment and visioning process, including

➤ a list of your accomplishments, strengths, and perceived weaknesses;

➤ an evaluation of your mental health, physical health, spirituality, relationships, finances, and career/business so you can assess your current results and uncover the beliefs that are creating them—and put into words new beliefs to take you where you want to go;

➤ a vision for your life in the areas of health, family, significant other, friends, career/business, spirituality, and finances; and

➤ a set of compelling goals for the next year and the next ninety days.

Of course, this is not a process you can complete in half an hour, or even a few days. It may take a week to finish the first part, what I call the True North exercises, and several more weeks to finalize your goals. Yet the word *finalize* may be misleading; you are never truly finished with goal setting. After all, life is not about checking items off a list; it's about learning and growing and continuing to expand your possibilities.

By using the Life Design Matrix, you'll make new decisions that will forever alter the course of your life. Even a one-degree change, over a period of time, will bring you to a totally different place. Imagine if a pilot made a one-degree change on his instruments for a flight going from Los Angeles to Paris. He could end up in Morocco! The same is true in your life. You're going to choose a new destination in the upcoming chapter, but for now let's dive into your present results and the beliefs that caused them.

It all begins with some serious reflection. If you're tempted not to assess your life because you think it's silly or a waste of time, you're simply bumping up against a belief. Be willing to set that aside for a while. When you're done with this book, you can always pick up that belief again, though I doubt you'll want to. The truth is that this is where the rubber meets the road. This is where you put everything you've learned into action to create the life of your dreams.

You'll start by taking inventory of your perceptions and beliefs about yourself, as well as where you are in your life today, itemizing your accomplishments, your strengths, and your perceived weaknesses. Start your lists simply by brainstorming, writing down whatever comes to mind, then moving on to the next list without worrying too much about making sure you've gotten "everything." Don't make this a mind-bending exercise; it should be fairly effortless. If you find that you get stuck, just set the lists aside and come back to them as thoughts occur to you. There's no time limit for completion.

Be aware that this process is not supposed to depress you. It's supposed to make you aware and to open up your mind to understanding how you create results in your life. You're welcome to use the aspects of this exercise that show you areas for improvement as motivation to get that ball rolling, but please don't see this as an opportunity to get mired in self-pity or regret. Look forward!

*Note: In the forms that follow, each provides twenty slots for you to fill. This is an arbitrary number. You don't have to list twenty items, nor are you limited to that number. Also know that these and all the forms in this book are available online at www.TheStreetKid.com. At the site, you can also subscribe at no coast to an e-newsletter ($97 value), which will both act as a reminder to help you stay on course and assist you in completing all the exercises by giving them to you in small, manageable pieces.*

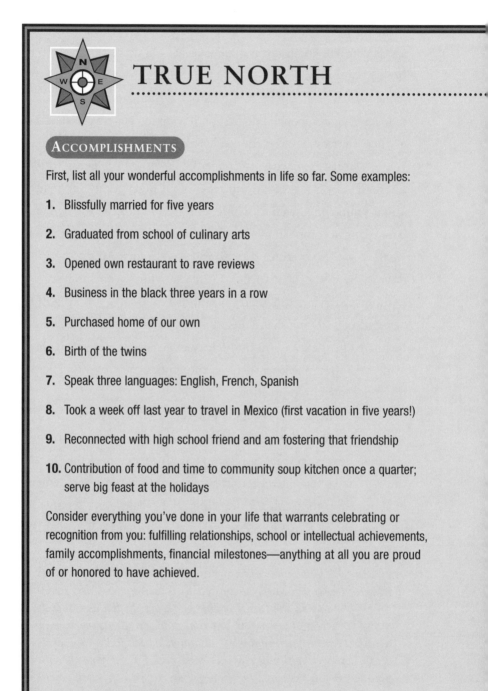

# TRUE NORTH

## ACCOMPLISHMENTS

First, list all your wonderful accomplishments in life so far. Some examples:

1. Blissfully married for five years

2. Graduated from school of culinary arts

3. Opened own restaurant to rave reviews

4. Business in the black three years in a row

5. Purchased home of our own

6. Birth of the twins

7. Speak three languages: English, French, Spanish

8. Took a week off last year to travel in Mexico (first vacation in five years!)

9. Reconnected with high school friend and am fostering that friendship

10. Contribution of food and time to community soup kitchen once a quarter; serve big feast at the holidays

Consider everything you've done in your life that warrants celebrating or recognition from you: fulfilling relationships, school or intellectual achievements, family accomplishments, financial milestones—anything at all you are proud of or honored to have achieved.

## ACCOMPLISHMENTS

1. _____
2. _____
3. _____
4. _____
5. _____
6. _____
7. _____
8. _____
9. _____
10. _____
11. _____
12. _____
13. _____
14. _____
15. _____
16. _____
17. _____
18. _____
19. _____
20. _____

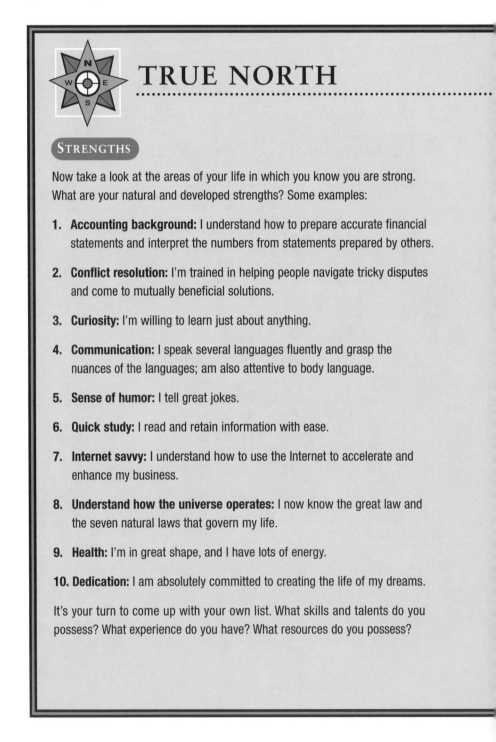

# TRUE NORTH

**STRENGTHS**

Now take a look at the areas of your life in which you know you are strong.
What are your natural and developed strengths? Some examples:

1. **Accounting background:** I understand how to prepare accurate financial
   statements and interpret the numbers from statements prepared by others.

2. **Conflict resolution:** I'm trained in helping people navigate tricky disputes
   and come to mutually beneficial solutions.

3. **Curiosity:** I'm willing to learn just about anything.

4. **Communication:** I speak several languages fluently and grasp the
   nuances of the languages; am also attentive to body language.

5. **Sense of humor:** I tell great jokes.

6. **Quick study:** I read and retain information with ease.

7. **Internet savvy:** I understand how to use the Internet to accelerate and
   enhance my business.

8. **Understand how the universe operates:** I now know the great law and
   the seven natural laws that govern my life.

9. **Health:** I'm in great shape, and I have lots of energy.

10. **Dedication:** I am absolutely committed to creating the life of my dreams.

It's your turn to come up with your own list. What skills and talents do you
possess? What experience do you have? What resources do you possess?

## STRENGTHS

1. _____
2. _____
3. _____
4. _____
5. _____
6. _____
7. _____
8. _____
9. _____
10. _____
11. _____
12. _____
13. _____
14. _____
15. _____
16. _____
17. _____
18. _____
19. _____
20. _____

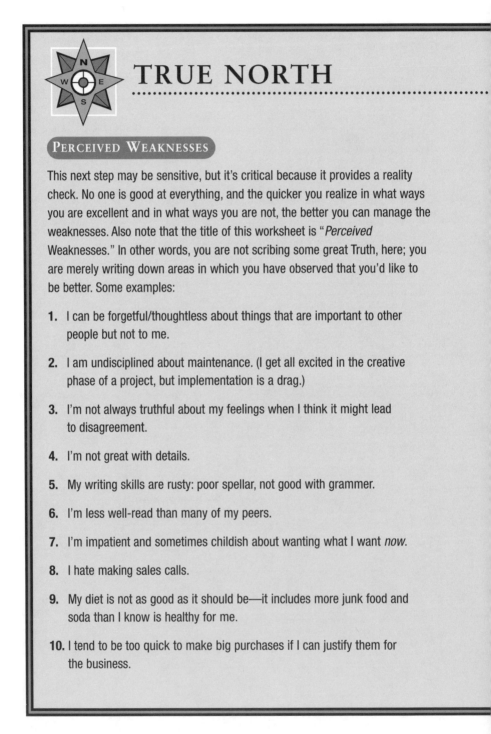

# TRUE NORTH

### PERCEIVED WEAKNESSES

This next step may be sensitive, but it's critical because it provides a reality check. No one is good at everything, and the quicker you realize in what ways you are excellent and in what ways you are not, the better you can manage the weaknesses. Also note that the title of this worksheet is "*Perceived Weaknesses.*" In other words, you are not scribing some great Truth, here; you are merely writing down areas in which you have observed that you'd like to be better. Some examples:

1. I can be forgetful/thoughtless about things that are important to other people but not to me.

2. I am undisciplined about maintenance. (I get all excited in the creative phase of a project, but implementation is a drag.)

3. I'm not always truthful about my feelings when I think it might lead to disagreement.

4. I'm not great with details.

5. My writing skills are rusty: poor spellar, not good with grammer.

6. I'm less well-read than many of my peers.

7. I'm impatient and sometimes childish about wanting what I want *now*.

8. I hate making sales calls.

9. My diet is not as good as it should be—it includes more junk food and soda than I know is healthy for me.

10. I tend to be too quick to make big purchases if I can justify them for the business.

## Perceived Weaknesses

1. _____
2. _____
3. _____
4. _____
5. _____
6. _____
7. _____
8. _____
9. _____
10. _____
11. _____
12. _____
13. _____
14. _____
15. _____
16. _____
17. _____
18. _____
19. _____
20. _____

## ASSESS YOUR CURRENT RESULTS

On the worksheets provided in the next few pages, you'll write a short evaluation of where you currently are in the categories of mental and physical health, relationships, spirituality, finances, and career/business.

Here's an example of a description of physical health: *My physical body is ten pounds overweight, and my food choices have not been the best. I have not exercised consistently in six months. My body fat is seventeen percent.* Consider what the person who wrote the paragraph above would have to believe about his or her health to have this result. Is it possible that the belief is it's okay to be ten pounds overweight and have seventeen percent body fat? Is this belief right or wrong?

Again, it's neither. The question is whether or not this is the desired result. If it is, then nothing needs to be done. If it's not, then the person needs to work on changing the belief so the result can be changed. The outward appearance or result is always a reflection of the inner belief and thinking.

Realize that whatever results you record had a cause at the subconscious level. For example, have you ever said to yourself, *I shouldn't eat this cake or cookie* or *I shouldn't do this or that,* and did it anyway? We all have. That is the power of your subconscious. It must keep you at exactly the weight you see yourself subconsciously.

Change the belief, and the thinking automatically changes. Change the thinking, and the action changes. Change the action, and the result changes. Therefore, depending on the results you personally want, align your beliefs with the desired outcome.

Continue now to the worksheets and begin to find your "true north." You can either write directly in this book, make copies of the worksheets, or go to www.TheStreetKid.com to download the forms. I recommend you do one of the latter and keep your completed worksheets for future reference, not only as you finish this book, but also for much later. I have notes like these from more than ten years ago, and they give me evidence of the awesome power of the mind to alter our destinies every time I look at them. We can accomplish so much when we choose to!

At the end of each assessment, be sure to write down what beliefs you have now about this part of your life. The beliefs will be evident based on your results. There's no denying your current results. They are what they are.

Again, it is really important not to get too caught up in your current results. Simply write them down, then move on. If you focus on them too much, all you do is reinforce and re-create the same belief. The only purpose of this exercise is to understand what you have been thinking and believing up to now.

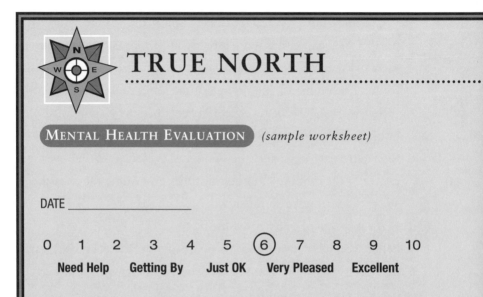

# TRUE NORTH

**MENTAL HEALTH EVALUATION** *(sample worksheet)*

DATE _____

0   1   2   3   4   5   ⑥   7   8   9   10

**Need Help**   **Getting By**   **Just OK**   **Very Pleased**   **Excellent**

My current Mental Health is:

*I'm doing pretty well. I have my days, but by and large my spirits are up and I'm an enjoyable person for others to be around. The one thing keeping me from feeling really excellent is that my grief over my father's death last year persists. I have a recurring dream where he is just out of my reach, and he can't hear or see me, but I can see him. The loss I feel over this is pervading the rest of my life to the point where, when I see my own children having fun with my husband, it is bittersweet. This keeps me from fully enjoying moments that should be wonderful for all of us— sometimes I tear up and have to turn away—and I think it's confusing for the kids.*

For this result to be present, my past programming or belief was:

*My father is gone and I'll never see him again. I won't ever be able to tell him I love him again. My children won't know their grandfather because he was taken from them so early in their lives, and I don't want to get all emotional in front of them because they're too young to understand what I'm going through.*

## MENTAL HEALTH EVALUATION

DATE _____

| 0 | 1 | 2 | 3 | 4 | 5 | 6 | 7 | 8 | 9 | 10 |
|---|---|---|---|---|---|---|---|---|---|---|
| **Need Help** | | **Getting By** | | **Just OK** | | **Very Pleased** | | **Excellent** | | |

My current Mental Health is:

_____

_____

_____

_____

_____

_____

_____

_____

For this result to be present, my past programming or belief was:

_____

_____

_____

_____

_____

# TRUE NORTH

**PHYSICAL HEALTH EVALUATION** *(sample worksheet)*

DATE _____

| 0 | 1 | 2 | 3 | 4 | 5 | 6 | 7 | (8) | 9 | 10 |
|---|---|---|---|---|---|---|---|---|---|---|
| **Need Help** | | **Getting By** | | **Just OK** | | **Very Pleased** | | **Excellent** | | |

My current Physical Health is:

*Really good. I'm exercising regularly, lifting weights and swimming several times a week, eating right, and taking my supplements. The best part is that I'm in better shape now than I was in my thirties. Look out fifty!*

For this result to be present, my past programming or belief was:

*I can be fit at any age. I love to eat healthfully and work out. I feel confident and sexy when I take care of my body. (I'm pretty happy with my 8, though I wouldn't mind kicking it up a notch.)*

## Physical Health Evaluation

DATE _____

| 0 | 1 | 2 | 3 | 4 | 5 | 6 | 7 | 8 | 9 | 10 |
|---|---|---|---|---|---|---|---|---|---|----|

**Need Help**   **Getting By**   **Just OK**   **Very Pleased**   **Excellent**

My current Physical Health is:

_____

_____

_____

_____

_____

_____

_____

_____

For this result to be present, my past programming or belief was:

_____

_____

_____

_____

_____

# TRUE NORTH

**SPIRITUALITY EVALUATION** *(sample worksheet)*

DATE _____

0   1   2   3   4   ⑤   6   7   8   9   10

**Need Help**   **Getting By**   **Just OK**   **Very Pleased**   **Excellent**

My current Spiritual Life is:

*Okay. I'm not very involved with religion but I feel the need for spiritual practice. My wife attends a church, but it's not a good match for me. It just feels like a social function more than a way to connect with God. So I get my connection with Spirit through nature, surfing specifically. That word "awesome" didn't come out of beach culture for nothing—the waves inspire me in ways that organized religion does not. But I don't have a lot of time for surfing, and I'd like it if our family was more connected spiritually. I'd like it if I was more connected spiritually.*

For this to be present, my past programming or belief was:

*I don't have the time to spend on this area of my life. Other things are always more pressing and important.*

## SPIRITUALITY EVALUATION

DATE _____

| 0 | 1 | 2 | 3 | 4 | 5 | 6 | 7 | 8 | 9 | 10 |
|---|---|---|---|---|---|---|---|---|---|----|

**Need Help**    **Getting By**    **Just OK**    **Very Pleased**    **Excellent**

My current Spiritual Life is:

_____

_____

_____

_____

_____

_____

_____

For this to be present, my past programming or belief was:

_____

_____

_____

_____

_____

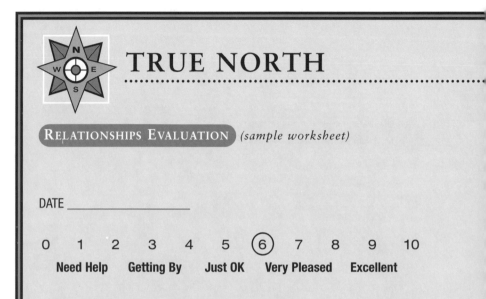

# TRUE NORTH

**RELATIONSHIPS EVALUATION** *(sample worksheet)*

DATE _____

| 0 | 1 | 2 | 3 | 4 | 5 | ⑥ | 7 | 8 | 9 | 10 |
|---|---|---|---|---|---|---|---|---|---|---|

**Need Help**    **Getting By**    **Just OK**    **Very Pleased**    **Excellent**

My current results in my Relationships are:

*Note: Describe each of your most important relationships individually.*

*Kids: The arrangement we have for seeing each other stinks. I have to drive two hours to pick them up then get to see them for only two days at a time. Given all that, we still have a great time together, and I feel like I'm able to contribute significantly to their parenting. They know how much I love them and I know they love me, too.*

*Terry: Things are rough. She doesn't want to bend on the visitation arrangement and still feels threatened by anything the kids and I do together that seems special and doesn't include her. Our conversations are civil but tense. I think she gets off on keeping this last bit of control over me.*

For this result to be present, my past programming or belief was:

*There's nothing I can do about the arrangement with the kids, I simply have to suck it up and deal with whatever life hands me. I'm not inclined to go out on a limb to help people who are trying to be difficult. Relationships can be complex, and especially so where women are involved.*

## RELATIONSHIPS EVALUATION

DATE _____

| 0 | 1 | 2 | 3 | 4 | 5 | 6 | 7 | 8 | 9 | 10 |
|---|---|---|---|---|---|---|---|---|---|----|

**Need Help        Getting By        Just OK        Very Pleased        Excellent**

My current results in my Relationships are:

*Note: Describe each of your most important relationships individually.*

_____

_____

_____

_____

_____

_____

_____

_____

For this result to be present, my past programming or belief was:

_____

_____

_____

_____

_____

# TRUE NORTH

**FINANCIAL EVALUATION** *(sample worksheet)*

DATE _____

| 0 | 1 | 2 | 3 | (4) | 5 | 6 | 7 | 8 | 9 | 10 |

**Need Help        Getting By        Just OK        Very Pleased        Excellent**

My current yearly income is $ *60,000* .

My current overall financial picture is:

*I am in over my head with unsecured debt. We live a little above our means, which results in a pretty nice lifestyle but lots of stress in trying to keep up with the bills every month. My income is decent, yet I think an increase would help relieve some of the pressure. Debt is the enemy of our future. It robs us of the ability to invest, and continuing offers of credit lure us into believing we can afford a lifestyle that's actually beyond our means right now. We need to STOP now and eliminate our debt so we can think farther ahead than just this month's bills. An increase in income won't make a dent unless we also alter our habits. When I get the raise I'm seeking, I want it to mean something!*

For this result to be present, my past programming or belief was:

*It's okay to accrue debt so long as I can foresee paying it off within three to five years. As long as we're able to meet our expenses every month, things are okay.*

## Financial Evaluation

DATE _____

| 0 | 1 | 2 | 3 | 4 | 5 | 6 | 7 | 8 | 9 | 10 |
|---|---|---|---|---|---|---|---|---|---|----|

**Need Help**    **Getting By**    **Just OK**    **Very Pleased**    **Excellent**

My current yearly income is $_____ .

My current overall financial picture is:

_____

_____

_____

_____

_____

_____

_____

_____

For this result to be present, my past programming or belief was:

_____

_____

_____

_____

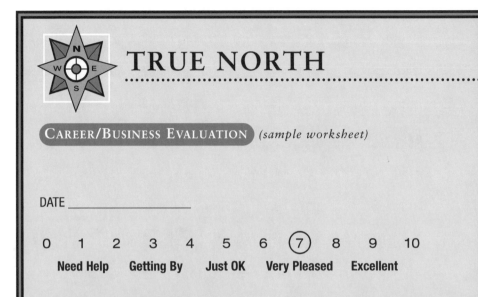

# TRUE NORTH

**CAREER/BUSINESS EVALUATION** *(sample worksheet)*

DATE _____

0    1    2    3    4    5    6    (7)    8    9    10

**Need Help**    **Getting By**    **Just OK**    **Very Pleased**    **Excellent**

The current results in my Career/Business are:

*We're making a reasonable profit for our fifth year in business, though I'd like to see more "big fish" type of clients come through our doors. Medical consulting as a field is still strong despite the economic downturn. Doctors always need help with the business side of their practices. I still enjoy the work I do and am getting more and more confident with making pitches to the bigger medical groups. My partners are enthusiastic and make valuable contributions to the growth of the business, although they're a little less interested in making the company start generating revenues that aren't directly dependent upon them.*

For this result to be present, my past programming or belief was:

*1) I need the full support of my partners to initiate new ideas in the company, because if the idea flops, I want it to have been with everyone's agreement so I don't get blamed. 2) I have to work harder to make more money. (Intellectually, I know this isn't true, but I behave as if it is, so I guess it's part of my programming.)*

## Career/Business Evaluation

DATE _____

| 0 | 1 | 2 | 3 | 4 | 5 | 6 | 7 | 8 | 9 | 10 |

**Need Help**   **Getting By**   **Just OK**   **Very Pleased**   **Excellent**

The current results in my Career/Business are:

_____

_____

_____

_____

_____

_____

_____

_____

For this result to be present, my past programming or belief was:

_____

_____

_____

_____

_____

### CHAPTER 6

# Design the Life of Your Dreams

*One of the greatest discoveries a man makes, one of his great surprises, is to find he can do what he was afraid he couldn't do.*

*—Henry Ford*

Several years ago, a gentleman hired my company to help him become more productive and figure out why he wasn't able to get himself motivated to work. He paid us fifty thousand dollars per month to coach him.

He had made hundreds of millions of dollars before he was thirty-five and hadn't worked in fifteen years. His biggest problem was that he did not know where he wanted to go in his career or what he wanted to do with his life. He'd become so complacent that he was driving himself crazy. He knew absolutely nothing of real value about himself, and although he was financially successful and had graduated from a top-tier university, he was lost as to who he really was and what he wanted to do with his life.

This man had no vision, no sense of purpose, no goals, so he dabbled in a number of things to occupy his time. He also felt that his life was quickly passing by, and he was unhappy. He had all the money he needed to play life's game at any level, yet he was bankrupt in every other way.

On the outside, it looked as if he had it all. After the first session with him, on his 120-foot yacht on a beautiful little island at the northern tip of the Grenadines, it became apparent that he was a brilliant super-achiever and with one phone call could be in touch with almost any person on this planet. Yet he was adrift because he had no real destination to move toward, both literally and figuratively. When he was tired of where he was on his yacht, he'd have it shipped to whichever part of the world he wanted to play in next and then hop on his jet to meet it there. Clearly, his biggest challenge was not financial but lack of purpose and meaning. He was utterly directionless.

Each of us must find our own direction. We need a vision for our lives, or else nothing we do means anything. This chapter is dedicated to helping you create a vision of possibility for your own life. For the time being, let's play "Just Imagine". . . If you could have it all, what would you do and be in your life? What would you buy, and what would you give? Whose counsel would you seek, what feats would you dare to accomplish, and where would you go? Just imagine your life, lived without limits.

God blessed you with a set of talents and unique qualities you must discover, develop, and exploit for yourself. All you can do is be who you are and become the best you possible. You must find that burning desire to do whatever it is that brings total joy in your heart.

Keep in mind you are not Michael Jordan or Barbra Streisand, so don't imagine their lives for yourself; create your own vision. That vision takes nothing away from what they have accomplished;

they are still superstars of incredible achievement in certain areas of their lives. Just understand that comparison is a fruitless exercise. It's all about personal choices, and that's where taking the time to design the life of *your* dreams comes into play.

Every person has uniqueness and the ability to create a masterpiece with the talents they possess. Many people just have not yet tapped into or really discovered this greatness. We have free will to do what we want, yet many people get caught up in belief systems that cause them pain and frustration. They hate their jobs. They don't get along with their spouses. And so on, leading lives, as the insightful writer Henry David Thoreau put it, of quiet desperation. What if it didn't have to be that way?

What if you could get up every morning and feel like you *get to,* instead of "have to," go to work? What if you could have a great relationship? We all spend so much time at jobs or in relationships that don't work for us. We should learn how to make them worth our life!

Have you ever fantasized about really having it all: money, health, spiritual connection, a job you love, and great relationships with your family, friends, your spouse and kids? Not only that, but having the balance to really enjoy your life?

There are so many questions to think about and so many decisions to make. But guess what? If you choose not to take the time to design and decide for yourself, circumstance or someone else will choose for you. This is not how your life was meant to be! **You deserve to decide for yourself exactly what and who you'll become and what you'll acquire along the way.** This book will guide you step by step on how to design the life of your dreams, and then how to live it. With your new plan, you'll have a road map and a mental picture of where you're headed. The journey becomes much easier once the destination is decided.

If you think it will come to you by lucky accident, you're making a grave error that will never allow you to really enjoy your life to the fullest. To have the type of life you deeply desire, you must first decide to make it that way and then define exactly what you want. Think of yourself as the captain of a ship, and it's time to set the course for your future destination. There are several ports of call where you need to stop on the way to the final destination, so you need a map to chart the course and set realistic timelines to reach each port. You also need to allow for possible storms and a host of other things that can, and probably will, take the ship off course once you set sail.

## GETTING PAST FEAR

The best acronym I've ever heard for fear is (F)alse (E)motions (A)ppearing (R)eal. And when we're caught in life's storm, fear sets in if we're unfamiliar with how we can best handle inclement weather. Great captains learn to chart their course and prepare as best as they can for the storms. They learn to use the wind to fill the sails, not destroy them. You can learn to be a great captain of yourself. It will take time and effort, but, honestly, no more time and effort than living a mediocre life. *It's up to you.*

Long ago I read about a study on goal setting, which revealed the number one reason most people don't write down their goals is fear of not achieving them. Don't let fear take you off course before you've even left the harbor!

For you to make headway in your journey, you must be totally honest about where you are today. That's why you completed the

True North exercise. It serves no purpose to lie to yourself about where you currently are. You must understand that where you are now is only the result of past thinking and planning or lack of it.

A new plan will bring new results. With the Life Design Matrix, these results will be carefully thought through and monitored so your outcome is consistent with your desires and dreams. So let's get started!

## COMPLETING THE LIFE DESIGN MATRIX

Using the worksheets on the next few pages, you'll be addressing the same general categories as you did in the True North exercise, with some specifics thrown in for good measure. For example, instead of having just one worksheet for relationships, you've got three: one for *family* (parents, siblings, children, extended family), one for *significant other,* and one for *friends.* This last category can include many different people, so take your time and write about the ones with whom you really want to have an outstanding relationship. Remember not to focus on the problems or challenges you may be facing now; instead, describe your vision if you could wave your magic wand and have your life any way you choose.

As you complete the worksheets, remember that the more specific you are the better! Also keep in this in mind: When you are setting the perfect life plan, *everything* must be clear and precise; exactly articulate your outcome, including the look and feel. The universe operates by exact and precise laws, and there's no room for ambiguity.

When you write the new beliefs you must develop (part of the exercise coming up), you must be precise again, and put them in the present tense. You may refer to your True North worksheets to glean beliefs you identified in that exercise; recasting a negative belief as a positive affirmation is the objective. Keep in mind how beliefs and habits are formed. Through repetition—affirmations on audiotape, visualization, and meditation—you'll begin to replace your old beliefs and habits with new ones. This will ensure you are using all available elements in your favor, both consciously and subconsciously.

In this section, not one word of negativity plays a role or has a purpose. Remember, you are designing your new life and a new way of seeing and expressing yourself. In addition, concern yourself only with what you want, not how to get it. Just use your imagination and create the picture in your mind. Don't shortchange yourself into writing what you *think* you can become and have. **The universe is infinite in supply, so really stretch yourself and go for your heart's desire.**

You'll start with your health, writing a description of your physical health if you could have it any way you want.

Write all this as if you have already achieved it, in the present tense, so your conscious mind can give these "instructions" to your subconscious. An example would be as follows: *I'm vibrant and feel that I'm in great shape. I'm working out regularly and also taking time for relaxation, so I have abundant energy every day! I love the way my body feels when I'm bicycling by the lake—my muscles all working together, my breathing deep and steady; it's so peaceful yet exhilarating . . .* and so on, giving the other particulars as if they were happening right now. (Sound familiar? This could be a script for the audiotape described in chapter 4.) This is just an example, of course. You need to use your own words so you become emotionally engaged—so you feel good and relate your words to being truly healthy.

In every case, you'll feel a little as if you're just "making it up." That's great! Employ your imagination! That's what visioning is all about. What if you don't have a romantic relationship right now? Fabulous! You get to create one just as you imagine it could be. What if you're in a dead-end job right now? Fine! You get to create a new vision of what fulfilling work would be for you. If you haven't developed any aspect of your life that's called for in these worksheets, now's your chance to envision something truly great. **The truth is that no matter what your current circumstances, if you can imagine something better for yourself, you can create it.** Suspend all skepticism and go for it![2]

When you finish the first worksheet, go on to the next. Feel free to add things as you go; mix it up. Progress in any order and then go back and forth to tweak as needed. As mentioned earlier, completing this part of the Life Design Matrix may extend over several days or more.

---

(2) The one possible exception is the spirituality worksheet. If you are an atheist, you may wish to forego this piece.

# MY VISION FOR THE LIFE OF MY DREAMS

• • • • • • • • • • • • • • • • • • • • • • • • • • • • • • • • • • • • • • • • • • • •

**HEALTH**

**Mental Health**

How do I approach life? What are my dominant emotions? What kind of mental activities do I engage in? How do I describe my intellect, my memory, my perception?

_____

_____

_____

_____

_____

**Physical Health**

How active am I? How do I feel? How much do I weigh? What is my body fat percentage? How do I see and feel about myself?

_____

_____

_____

_____

_____

My new belief that is now created to achieve my optimal health is:

*(E.g., As I'm getting older, I am in better shape than ever before, and I feel great!)*

_____

_____

# MY VISION FOR THE LIFE OF MY DREAMS

### FAMILY

How do I interact with each member of my family? How do I feel when I'm around them? What do I give to them? What do they give to me?

_____

_____

_____

_____

_____

_____

_____

_____

My new belief that is now created to achieve my ideal family:

*(E.g., I feel dad's love surrounding me every day.)*

_____

_____

_____

_____

_____

_____

_____

# MY VISION FOR THE LIFE OF MY DREAMS

### SIGNIFICANT OTHER

What is life like with this romantic partner? What do we enjoy together?
What kinds of emotions does this relationship foster? What does this person
bring out in me? What do I give to the relationship? What do we create
together? What would happen during an ideal day with this person?

_____

_____

_____

_____

_____

_____

_____

_____

My new belief that is now created to achieve the relationship of my
dreams with my significant other is:

*(E.g., Lou and I are lovingly connected, passionately*

*attracted, and growing in our relationship every day.)*

_____

_____

_____

_____

_____

_____

_____

# MY VISION FOR THE LIFE OF MY DREAMS

FRIENDSHIP WITH _____

What makes this friendship special? What activities do we share? What topics do we discuss? How do we help each other? What does this person bring out in me, and what do I bring out in him or her?

_____

_____

_____

_____

_____

_____

_____

_____

My new belief that is now created to achieve the friendship of my dreams with _____ is:

*(E.g., We are building a friendship for a lifetime.)*

_____

_____

_____

_____

_____

_____

_____

# MY VISION FOR THE LIFE OF MY DREAMS

### CAREER/BUSINESS

What kind of services do I provide? How much am I paid? What is my work environment? How many hours a week do I devote to professional pursuits? Who are my colleagues or clients? Why do I love this line of work? What does it add to my life? In what ways am I able to contribute to others through my work? In what way is this work important?

_____

_____

_____

_____

_____

_____

_____

_____

My new belief that is now created to achieve the satisfaction and success in the career/business that I desire is:

*(E.g., My business is generating $250,000/year in profit.*

*Business is flowing to our company in abundance.)*

_____

_____

_____

_____

_____

## MY VISION FOR THE LIFE OF MY DREAMS

SPIRITUALITY

What kind of relationship do I have with my god? How connected do I feel? What kind of spiritual practice do I engage in, if any? What do my religious or spiritual beliefs bring to my life? How do I experience spirituality? Are there particular places or actions that help me feel inspired and uplifted?

_____

_____

_____

_____

_____

_____

_____

_____

_____

My new belief that is now created to achieve the spirituality I desire is:
*(E.g., I feel God's presence in my life wherever I go, and I feel totally connected.)*

_____

_____

_____

_____

_____

_____

# MY VISION FOR THE LIFE OF MY DREAMS

**FINANCES**

What is my approach to money management? What is my annual income? How much do I have invested and saved? Do I have any debt? Who benefits from my financial situation? How does it benefit me?

_____

_____

_____

_____

_____

_____

_____

_____

_____

My new belief that is now created to achieve the financial outcome I desire is:

*(E.g., I am debt-free and earning $100,000 a year. I love*

*having extra cash in the bank!)*

_____

_____

_____

_____

_____

_____

Take some time to imagine if all this was really possible. How would you feel to achieve the life about which you just wrote? Really take this in, because it is a huge thing to embrace. Getting emotionally charged about this "new" life is the best fuel you can have. You must create a burning desire to really go for it.

It's tempting to think, *Well, that was interesting, but it'll never happen.* There are plenty of people who will tell you that this type of thinking and planning is a bunch of bull. I would challenge you to look at results and not opinions. Do your own homework.

I can assure you that when I started doing this twenty years ago, I was skeptical. But one thing I couldn't deny was the fact that the teachers who taught me the techniques in this book had done their homework and were achieving many of the results I wanted to create. What did I have to lose? At the time I was introduced to the world of personal development, I was earning ten thousand dollars a year. I hadn't been educated beyond high school, and I became a student of human potential.

Today, I'm living proof of what you can achieve by using these principles. There's no doubt in my mind that all I have created, from my family to my financial wealth to my absolute faith in God, has been a direct result of the exact steps you're taking right now to complete your Life Design Matrix. I am truly honored and excited to share with you what I know to be true out of my own results, not some unproven theory or hypothesis.

And, by the way, there are many people just like me—and just like you—who are putting these principles to work for them.

## THE LIFE YOU WILL CREATE

Now that you've written about each aspect individually, it's time to create one cohesive document that incorporates your entire vision onto one or two pages. Again, spend some time with this. You might write your first draft in just a few minutes, but then let it rest and tweak it so it flows and makes sense. This will serve as your quick reference for your destination, the life you're building by design.

As an example, this is my latest text, which I wrote for myself about eight months ago in 2002. Know that I'll be updating this at the end of the year and making it even more precise.

### *My Life and Living It at the Summit*

*I am living the life of my dreams. I am extremely grateful for all that God has provided me, and I put all of my faith in his power and infinite intelligence.*

*I am an excellent father to Keenan and Noah, and I love being a part of their growth, development, and lives.*

*I am enjoying great relationships with all members of my family.*

*I am enjoying an abundance of energy, and I am so healthy and happy both physically and mentally.*

*I am enjoying an outstanding relationship with Maria, and we are growing beautifully and lovingly together.*

*My net worth is now $———— and I am now earning $———— a year for my services as an author, speaker, consultant, and entrepreneur.*

*I am debt-free, and money is flowing to me in abundance. I have $———— cash in the bank and investments.*

*I am happily giving $———— a year to charities.*

*I am disciplined and have excellent willpower to keep me focused on my dream life.*

*I am very blessed and grateful for my whole life!*

You see that this doesn't have to be some masterwork of prose or poetry. **Just write with your heart and your imagination engaged.** I suggest you collect your new belief statements on the worksheet provided, then transfer your vision to a one-page document you can post in your office at home or work, put in your organizer, or type into the screen saver on your computer. Keep this vision accessible to you as much as possible.

## MY LIFE AND LIVING IT AT THE SUMMIT

### CHAPTER 7

# Use the Magic of Goal Setting

*Destiny is not a matter of chance, but a matter of choice.*
*It is not a thing to be waited for; it is a thing to be achieved.*
*—William Jennings Bryant*

You may have heard about a study of alumni ten years out of Harvard.[3] An astonishing eighty-three percent left with their degrees and had no goals at all. Fourteen percent had defined specific objectives for themselves, but they never wrote them down.

The group with goals earned an average of three times the income of the group without them. Interesting, I think. Now here comes the blow-away. The remaining three percent of the graduates who had specific goals *and wrote them down* earned an average of ten times what the eighty-three-percent group did.

Let's do the math. At this writing, we know a Harvard grad earns an average of $121,979 in the first year of work, and I'm

(3) This story has been circulating in the personal development community for so long that it's become something of an urban legend. Although I've been unable to personally verify the study, it certainly makes a point that I do know is true without question: Setting goals hones our focus, gives us direction, and makes it far more likely that we'll actually live the life of our dreams rather than just drift along on whatever whim our circumstances present. Goal setting has been one of the most powerful tools I've learned in my life, second only to visualization.

certain it goes up from there. Just in the first five years, the decision not to write specific goals down can cost these people millions.

We have to assume the same principle is true for all of us. Going to Harvard may be an excellent predictor of financial gains, but not all of us had that chance. But you do have the chance *right now* to multiply your earning power, not to mention your ability to create anything else in your life that you desire.

## WHAT IS A GOAL?

When I refer to goals, they're not generalized desires, such as "I want more money," or "I want to be happy." I'm referring to exact, specific outcomes: results you can get your head and emotions around. I'm talking about the first step in moving toward the life of your dreams.

Consider the story of Nate Brooks, who was born and raised in the projects of the South Bronx and Harlem. His father was an alcoholic and died from cirrhosis of the liver, his mother did not speak a word of English, and his brother was a drug user who spent most of his time in prison.

You probably wouldn't be surprised if I told you that I met Nate in my days with the gang, that we got together over some great hustle. But that's not the case; I met Nate through RE/MAX, where he was *kicking butt* in the real estate market. You see, when Nate was young he decided to create a life different from the one into which he was born. He decided he wanted more, and his conditions wouldn't determine what he'd become or have. He did it strictly on the straight and narrow path: Not only did Nate get out of the projects, but he also graduated from the U.S. Merchant Marine Academy with a bachelor's degree in marine engineering (with honors, no less), then earned his master's degree in nuclear engineering in just one year at the Massachusetts Institute of Technology. He then worked for a year before going on to earn an MBA from Harvard.

Today, Nate lives in northern California and is among the top one percent of real estate agents in the country. He and his family average six weeks of vacation a year and live a life of abundance. He's also an avid bowler, getting in fifty to seventy-five games a week while he manages three businesses as an entrepreneur.

Nate will tell you that he designed and planned his life almost *exactly* the way I'm teaching you in this book. Apropos of his Harvard degree, he calls his version of the Life Design Matrix his "Personal Life and Business Plan."

Remember, the universe works with exact order and precision, not in ambiguity. Nate defined exactly what he wanted to create, outlined the steps to get him there, then went for it. As you work on your goals in this chapter, keep in mind that specificity is your greatest ally. Imagine if former president John F. Kennedy had said, "Let's see if we can get someone close to the moon." Instead, he told us,

First, I believe that this nation should commit itself to achieving the goal, before this decade is out, of landing a man on the moon and returning him safely to the earth. No single space project in this period will be more impressive to mankind, or more important for the long-range exploration of space; and none will be so difficult or expensive to accomplish. We propose to accelerate the development of the appropriate lunar space craft. We propose to develop alternate liquid and solid fuel boosters, much larger than any now being developed, until certain which is superior. We propose additional funds for other engine development and for unmanned explorations—explorations which are particularly important for one purpose which this nation will never overlook: the survival of the man who first makes this daring flight. But in a very real sense, it will not be one man going to the moon—if we make this judgment affirmatively, it will be an entire nation. For all of us must work to put him there. (Special Message to the Congress on Urgent National Needs, delivered in person before a joint session of Congress, May 25, 1961.)

Talk about exactitude!

Let's take one giant step toward your greatest leap. Create a masterpiece by putting your goals in writing with specificity and conviction. But before you make a commitment to any particular set of goals, make a commitment to yourself. If you're determined to live the life of your dreams, read and sign (and mean it!) the agreement on the next page.

## BINDING AGREEMENT WITH
## ME, MYSELF, AND I

DATE _____

I, the undersigned, commit and agree to furnish all materials and labor necessary to design and create the LIFE OF MY DREAMS.

I hereby commit to doing whatever it takes without being dishonest or deceitful to achieve the greatness I know is within me.

I will pay the necessary price to reach my life's dream and destiny, because I know not fulfilling my destiny will leave me feeling short-changed in my life.

I understand that my life's design plan is going to be reached one step at a time, with each step bringing me closer to the LIFE OF MY DREAMS.

I will not settle for anything other than achieving the LIFE OF MY DREAMS.

I have the power, I have the knowledge, and I have what it takes.


_____

Signature of Commitment


_____

Date

## SET YOUR ONE-YEAR GOALS

Now you're ready to begin putting your one-year goals in writing. I've found that what works best for me is first setting my overall life goal, which is also my master vision and overview. (If you completed the exercises in the previous chapter, then you have done this already, too, and you'll want to have them handy as you complete this next section.) I then develop that vision into my one-year goals with specific monthly, weekly, and daily goals and actions that move me in that direction for each section of my life.

> *I am the architect of myself.*
>
> *—Carl Rodgers*

If you have difficulty constructing the action plan part of the following worksheets ("Here's What I'm Doing Now to Achieve My Goals"), remember what you've already learned in this book. You'll probably need to focus first on reprogramming specific beliefs. Once that work is done, look to your role models. In every part of our culture, there's somebody who dominates. You have access to people who are excelling at something you're not. Find out what they do, how they do it, then copy what you need and add your own twist and genius to it.

If you feel that you need one-on-one coaching, consider recruiting a mentor or exploring some of the services The Street Kid Company has to offer (www.TheStreetKid.com). There have been several people in my life who have assisted me in this way. In business, I've had many guides as well. I can't imagine having created my level of success in real estate without several key men guiding me.

Choose someone you respect and who has accomplished what you're setting out to do. Then just ask. Some people let their fear of rejection or of being an imposition get in the way of posing this simple question: "Would you be willing to mentor me?" Of course, there's a little more to that conversation, including telling the prospective mentor why it will benefit him or her, too. You can propose that you meet at the mentor's office so he or she isn't inconvenienced, you can contribute your talents free of charge to the mentor's pet project, you can pick up the dry cleaning—whatever it is, think of something that will be of service to the mentor. How to begin? How about something like this:

> I want to accomplish _____, and I respect the results you've produced in your life. Would you be willing to help by meeting with me once a week so I can learn from your achievements? I'd like to make it worth your while by _____. Does a mentor relationship with me sound like something you'd enjoy?

If you have difficulty with any aspect of this goal-setting process, just set it aside for a day then come back to it. Don't feel that you have to complete these worksheets in one frantic, fifteen-minute scribbling session. You may need to do research, even spend some cash to figure out what the proper steps will be. You certainly will need to spend some time in serious reflection. Don't rush this process, but don't dawdle, either. Your life awaits.

# MY ONE-YEAR GOALS

From _____ to _____

### MENTAL HEALTH

- _____

- _____

- _____

- _____

- _____

- _____

Here's what I'm now doing to achieve my goals:

- _____

- _____

- _____

- _____

- _____

Once your yearly goals are written, break them down into achievable monthly, weekly, and daily routines and activities like baby steps. Use your calendar, day planner, or other organizing tool to record these activities and keep track of your progress.

## MY ONE-YEAR GOALS

From _____ to _____

**PHYSICAL HEALTH**

- _____
- _____
- _____
- _____
- _____
- _____

Here's what I'm now doing to achieve my goals:

- _____
- _____
- _____
- _____
- _____
- _____

Once your yearly goals are written, break them down into achievable monthly, weekly, and daily routines and activities like baby steps. Use your calendar, day planner, or other organizing tool to record these activities and keep track of your progress.

# MY ONE-YEAR GOALS

From _____ to _____

**FINANCES**

- _____
- _____
- _____
- _____
- _____
- _____

Here's what I'm now doing to achieve my goals:

- _____
- _____
- _____
- _____
- _____
- _____

Once your yearly goals are written, break them down into achievable monthly, weekly, and daily routines and activities like baby steps. Use your calendar, day planner, or other organizing tool to record these activities and keep track of your progress.

## MY ONE-YEAR GOALS

From _____ to _____

**SPIRITUALITY**

- _____
- _____
- _____
- _____
- _____
- _____

Here's what I'm now doing to achieve my goals:

- _____
- _____
- _____
- _____
- _____
- _____

Once your yearly goals are written, break them down into achievable monthly, weekly, and daily routines and activities like baby steps. Use your calendar, day planner, or other organizing tool to record these activities and keep track of your progress.

# MY ONE-YEAR GOALS

From _____ to _____

FAMILY

•  _____

•  _____

•  _____

•  _____

•  _____

•  _____

Here's what I'm now doing to achieve my goals:

•  _____

•  _____

•  _____

•  _____

•  _____

•  _____

Once your yearly goals are written, break them down into achievable monthly, weekly, and daily routines and activities like baby steps. Use your calendar, day planner, or other organizing tool to record these activities and keep track of your progress.

## MY ONE-YEAR GOALS

From _____ to _____

**SIGNIFICANT OTHER**

- _____
- _____
- _____
- _____
- _____
- _____

Here's what I'm now doing to achieve my goals:

- _____
- _____
- _____
- _____
- _____
- _____

Once your yearly goals are written, break them down into achievable monthly, weekly, and daily routines and activities like baby steps. Use your calendar, day planner, or other organizing tool to record these activities and keep track of your progress.

# MY ONE-YEAR GOALS

From _____ to _____

**CHILDREN**

• _____

• _____

• _____

• _____

• _____

• _____

Here's what I'm now doing to achieve my goals:

• _____

• _____

• _____

• _____

• _____

Once your yearly goals are written, break them down into achievable monthly, weekly, and daily routines and activities like baby steps. Use your calendar, day planner, or other organizing tool to record these activities and keep track of your progress.

## MY ONE-YEAR GOALS

From _____ to _____

**CAREER/BUSINESS**

- _____
- _____
- _____
- _____
- _____
- _____

Here's what I'm now doing to achieve my goals:

- _____
- _____
- _____
- _____
- _____
- _____

Once your yearly goals are written, break them down into achievable monthly, weekly, and daily routines and activities like baby steps. Use your calendar, day planner, or other organizing tool to record these activities and keep track of your progress.

Legendary basketball coach John Wooden said he used to spend more than one hour of planning for every ten minutes of actual practice. With this formula, he won more NCAA basketball championships than any coach ever has. The reason is that his players were doing what they were supposed to be doing during practice instead of using the time to figure it out. By the way, those practices were short so his players could do other important things like study and enjoy college. Wooden believed in getting the most out of his players not only on the court, but also in life.

Once you have gotten your own details figured out and put in writing, you simply follow the plan and modify as needed. Most people try to ride and build the bike at the same time, which is frustrating and nearly impossible to achieve. Become a planner, not a complainer.

*If you add a little to a little, and then do it again, soon that little shall be much.*

*—Hesiod*

It's easier to adjust for a week's worth of errors than a month or two, so set aside a monthly, weekly, and daily block of time to review and plan where you are compared to where you want to be. I use an hour every Sunday to plan my week and evaluate the previous week.

It's critical to always have your goal forms and life planning documents at your fingertips, as accessible to you as your regular planner, whether it's electronic or on paper. Like most people, I have a list a mile long of things to accomplish—all of which have grown directly out of my goals—and I also have my "daily winning plan" to follow. This is the plan I'm using right now:

*John's Winning Daily Program & Plan*

➤ *Take action!*

➤ *Meditate (30 min.)*

➤ *Exercise (1 hr.)*

➤ *Visualize: Review goals (20 min.)*

➤ *Learn: Read a book, listen to a tape, or watch a video (30 min. to 1 hr.)*

➤ *Eat healthy, fresh foods*

➤ *Appreciate, love, be grateful, have fun*

To fuel action on your goals, take some time to consider how achieving them makes you feel. How will you act, walk, and talk when you achieve each goal? What will you do with your new abundant life? Come up with as many positive reasons and anchors as you can for achieving your goal to fuel you to do your best.

Some people are fueled by fear of failing and others by the quest to be the best they can be. Personally, I don't use the prospect of negative consequences to motivate me, but I acknowledge this could be a key component for you. If you know that moving away from failure is a prime incentive for you, use it. **Use whatever works for you and go for gold.** Just don't sit on the sidelines waiting for things to change. Take charge and make your dreams come true.

# Life Design Matrix Checklist

### Chapter 5

☐ Make a list of accomplishments, strengths, and perceived weaknesses.

☐ True North: Assess current results and beliefs.

### Chapter 6

☐ Clarify a vision for health, family, significant other, friendships, career/business, spirituality, and finances.

### Chapter 7

☐ Commit to creating the life of my dreams: Read and sign "Binding Agreement With Me, Myself, and I."

☐ Set life goals.

☐ Set goals for one year and determine actions for the next month, week, and day.

### Implement the Plan

☐ Get to work on adopting new beliefs (use methods in chapter 4).

☐ Take action and make course corrections as needed.

☐ Celebrate achievements!

### A Gift for You!

If you'd benefit from weekly encouragement and review—and who wouldn't?—receive The Street Kid's weekly e-newsletter (a $97 value) by subscribing at www.TheStreetKid.com. Each step is broken into simple weekly tasks. Think what a difference a year of focus and accountability will make!

**PART III**

# Take Your Life to the Next Level

### CHAPTER 8

# Foster the Seven Power Factors

*Power doesn't have to show off. Power is confident, self-assuring, self-starting and self-stopping, self-warming and self-justifying. When you have it, you know it.*

—*Ralph Ellison*

Every successful entrepreneur, company, entertainer, or athlete has several key ingredients, which I call "power factors," that are critical for playing and achieving at the highest level. Some people have more of one than another, and that's perfectly okay. It's your responsibility to take notice of what you have, what you can develop (strengths), and what you must manage (weaknesses). The power factors are:

*Persistence • Attitude*

*Discipline • Vision • Purpose*

*Focus • Action*

Let's look at what each one means and begin to develop the mind-set of the high achiever.

## 1. PERSISTENCE

You've probably heard of the incredibly popular and profitable *Chicken Soup for the Soul* series of books. When the first collection of stories was published, it was a near-instant success, but this belies the fact that there's a story of amazing persistence behind it. The creators of the series, Mark Victor Hansen and Jack Canfield, approached 141 publishers with their book idea before one agreed to give it a try. Think about this for a moment. That means 141 rejection letters, 141 people who told them "I don't want your book," 141 people who passed. It was a costly error for those less-than-visionary publishers; the pair has since sold more than 75 million books, garnering unimagined profits for the lone publisher who was willing to take a chance.

> Those who are blessed with the most talent don't necessarily outperform everyone else. It's the people with follow-through who excel.
>
> —Mary Kay Ash

When should you give up? When do you throw in the towel and abandon the journey, the mission, the purpose, and your dreams? When would you give up on teaching a baby to walk? Toddlers are not very good at it when they start; in fact, they wobble around, have to hang onto other people and furniture to stand up, and fall down all the time. But do you let that discourage you?

What about a business venture? Finding the love of your life? A lost brother or sister? Will you let short-term setbacks and missteps deter you from your dream?

Some things are even worth dying for; others must be handled with caution because you might be better off moving in a different direction. For example, if you were heavily invested in a sector of the stock market that was proving to be a dog, all the persistence in the world could leave you bankrupt. On the other hand, if you were trying to close a deal that could catapult your company to the next level, you'd probably be wise to do whatever it took (without being dishonest) to get the deal done.

Finding different ways to accomplish something is a critical virtue for success. Trying all you can and never quitting until every last possibility is exhausted is the quality that separates the leaders and winners from the mediocre. British leader Winston Churchill, by refusing to back down in the face of Hitler's advancing army despite a seemingly irresistible force poised to overtake him, personified persistence. His steadfastness influenced the future of the entire free world, and his eloquence moved the people of England, when he plainly stated the time to quit: *never, never, never.* He didn't mean that we ought to be irrationally stubborn, however, just that we ought to stand by our convictions so long as they continue to be both sensible and noble.

> *Never give in—never, never, never, never, in nothing great or small, large or petty, never give in except to convictions of honor and good sense. Never yield to force; never yield to the apparently overwhelming might of the enemy.*
>
> —*Winston Churchill*

Of course, persistence comes in many forms, as do "enemies." In business, your opponent may be a company competing for your market share; it may also be something less obvious, such as flaws in management or strategy, or even your team's perception of how long it will take to get something done. In a relationship, the enemy could be your fears, anger, or neglect. In your finances, you could be battling debt or cash-flow problems. Churchill tells us not to fold under these pressures. Not to fold under any pressures.

Think that's too much to ask? Perhaps we can take a lesson from a venerable senior citizen, the late Colonel Sanders of Kentucky Fried Chicken. At the age of sixty-five, when he wanted to start KFC, he began by driving from town to town offering to sell his "secret recipe" to restaurants. He frequently slept in his car and almost exclusively ate his chicken for sustenance. He achieved his objective only after he had approached 1,009 people. The 1,010th finally said yes, the Colonel's chicken was indeed "finger-lickin' good" enough to sell to the public. The rest is fast-food history.

Thomas Edison failed nine thousand times before he perfected his invention of the light bulb. (Was he distressed by the number of failed attempts? He is reputed to have said, "I'm glad to have found 8,999 ways to not invent the light bulb!") He later went on to secure 1,093 patents, more than any other person in U.S. history.

What about Michael Jordan? The first time he tried out for the varsity team at his high school, he didn't make the cut. That fueled him to become a better player—practicing every day until the next year's tryouts—and ultimately, he became the best ever in the sport. He simply never quit.

There are multitudes of stories like this, enough to fill a library. Helen Keller, Mother Teresa, the astronauts of Apollo 13, Ray Kroc, Sir Edmund Hillary and, yes, Winston Churchill, too. There are so many others, both famous and not. You have probably met someone in your own life who has summoned this resource, refused to quit, and accomplished something great because of it. **I don't know of any other characteristic more important to achieving success than persistence.**

Yet the value in persistence is not so much the great things we can accomplish. Instead, it's the experiences we gather along the way, the ups and downs—those are the gifts. We think when we're young that the goal is what we want, but it's really who we become along the way and the experiences we gather during the journey that bring us joy. What's more desirable: to have someone give you a million dollars, or to know you have earned it yourself? It might be great to have someone give you a million bucks, but the character you'd create by earning it would be the greater gift. Likewise, a parent's joy isn't in the "finished product" of an adult child; it's in raising the child, helping another person develop, shaping the young person's values and ideals, and being with him or her through all phases of life. It's all the good memories and the trials and tribulations that we remember when our final breath is near.

## 2. ATTITUDE

One of the great mysteries for us to uncover is attitude. Why are some people always in a good mood and enjoying a great outlook, while others are exactly the opposite? How much of attitude is genetic versus a learned behavior?

I'm blessed with a great attitude that I believe I've developed by choice. Education has given me the understanding that I actually have chosen this attitude. I'm not talking about school; I'm referring to the understanding of self. You have the choice every day about how you're going to spend your time and how you choose to react to whatever happens.

In any situation, you have a decision to make. You can either give circumstances total control over you and allow them to rob you of your energy, or you can take control of them and propel yourself forward. Remember how my friend Nate Brooks beat the odds, emerging from the projects to become extraordinarily well educated and an incredibly successful businessman. It was his *attitude* that propelled him forward; he would still be living in the South Bronx (or worse) if he had decided to let his circumstances control him.

You are blessed with the ability to wake up each day and decide your attitude. **Each circumstance gives you the opportunity to choose how you'll react to it.** It's never the circumstance that controls you. It's your choice each and every time.

As you now know, seeing both sides of everything is using one of nature's laws, the law of polarity. Choosing to be positive and moving forward is simply a matter of decision and attention.

Not only can you choose your own attitude, but you can make choices about the attitudes of those around you. I don't mean that you can influence people to be positive by being positive yourself, although that's true to a degree; I mean that you can be selective about the people with whom you spend your time, and therefore your life. Personally, I don't allow negative people to infiltrate my mind or life. It's not that I won't be sensitive to someone being sad because of a particular event or a tragedy. I'm saying I avoid people who cannot see the good in anything, people I call "psychic vampires."

One member of my family has the uncanny ability to see only what's wrong with something. I once offered to take her on a cruise, first-class airfare included. I was shocked (or maybe not) when she started to complain about the packing, the time to fly, the heat, five different ports of call, and a layover. I quickly agreed and suggested that maybe we should do it at another time. Thank goodness she also agreed. Shortly after I returned, she experienced a feeling of self-pity for not having taken me up on the offer. I felt relieved! It wouldn't have been much of a vacation with such a complainer on board.

Attitude is so important. It's the wind in your sails. It's the single most important part of being totally happy. It's also one hundred percent in your own control.

Every once in awhile, one of my kids cops an attitude I don't appreciate. I point this out to them along with the consequence of continuing this attitude. We talk about whose attitude it is and who can change it. In almost every case the outlook and behavior change.

For example, let's say my boys come home from school and they start to whine: "I don't waaaant to do my chores."

My question to them: "Why don't you want to do your chores?"

Predictably, they answer, "I don't know," so I ask, "Is this attitude going to benefit you, or is this attitude going to cause consequences you don't want?"

Keenan and Noah are both smart kids, and it doesn't take long before they realize the attitude isn't going to get them anywhere they want to go, so they tell me, "It's going to cause consequences I don't want."

"Whose choice is it to change your attitude?"

"Mine."

"And if you don't change it," I ask, "what will the consequences be?" They understand what kind of consequences come with refusing to do something, usually spending some time in their rooms alone, what is often called a "time out." And they always have the option of accepting those consequences—they always have a choice. But usually, they opt for changing their attitude.

After they tell me what they think the consequences will be, I ask, "When do you think it would be a good time to choose the attitude that will get the results you want?"

*"Right now."*

If my children can learn this lesson so quickly, I have absolute confidence that adults can apply it just as fast. I truly believe that you can condition yourself, if you're aware, to control your attitude and thereby direct your life.

## 3. DISCIPLINE

Discipline is to your life's success what carbon is to steel: You need the one to have the other. The ability to give yourself a command and follow it is imperative in order to achieve the life of your dreams.

You expect your children and your employees to be disciplined, and you must expect it from yourself. Without discipline, stuff just waits and gathers dust. Once you have decided and determined what you want to achieve, a pragmatic and disciplined approach must be part of the path to achieving the desired outcome.

Greatness takes time, and patience and consistency determine the outcome.

Your willpower and true desire play a huge role in your discipline. If there's no real emotion and benefit in the outcome you want, then you won't pay the price of following through with what you need in order to achieve your dream life.

The times when you don't feel like doing what's needed are when it counts the most. The way to develop the ability to get up and do it anyway is through sheer determination and desire. Gold medallist Peter Vidmar is known to say that to be a champion he had to do only two things: Work out when he wanted to and work out when he didn't.

The same holds true with regard to discipline and your own goals. Even though you may not want to do something, if you know it's important and part of your plan, you must do it anyway. With time, you'll develop a skill and habit for short-circuiting the temptation to be lazy and instead suck it up and take action.

There's a saying that the difference between being interested in a result and committed to that result is that when you're interested, you do what's convenient; when you're committed, you do whatever it takes. **Are you interested in or committed to creating the life of your dreams?**

> *Most people tiptoe through life, hoping to make it safely to death.*
>
> *—Earl Nightingale*

By the way, it's now four in the morning as I'm editing the book you're reading. I went to bed at eleven and woke up at 2:50 A.M., got up and came to my office to edit. Trust me, it was very cozy and warm in my bed, but I'm committed to the outcome you now have in your hands. Without that level of effort on my part, this book would never get done. *Be a doer, not a talker.*

## 4. & 5. VISION AND PURPOSE

Of what importance is all this planning and designing if there's no purpose to it all?

One of the greatest motivators for each one of us is the question of why. Why should I? Why am I?

Deep inside each of us we yearn for the true meaning in our life. What do I stand for? What do I believe in? For what importance am I here on earth? These are all questions worthy of serious consideration and contemplation.

I believe each of us has a need to belong and fit into the whole. I also believe we all need and want to contribute as much as we can. In truth, we are all part of the whole, although some people feel more connected than others.

Determine your life's purpose. Ask yourself, *What is one thing that if I don't do it, I will feel my life has been a waste of time?* There are visions for each part of your life and together they'll create the life of your dreams. It doesn't matter whether you contribute your life to being a great mom, husband, athlete, or businessperson. **The essence of who you are and what you are is always for fuller expression and expansion.** People become lethargic and sick when they don't feel that there's purpose or meaning for their existence.

What's the purpose of your life? How will you derive the greatest fulfillment as you experience this journey you're on? The time to fully enjoy yourself and create a masterpiece is now, not sometime in the future. All we have is now.

Determine the vision you see for your life, and immediately do something to move yourself toward that frontier.

## 6. & 7. FOCUS AND ACTION

All the written plans in the world, all the inscribed goals, dreams, desires, and the rest of the lot, won't make even good wallpaper if the first action isn't taken.

There are so many brilliant people out there who analyze and plan and never get to first base because they don't get out and *do*. The focus is the goal; the action is where the real difference is.

So many people are afraid of making mistakes that they paralyze themselves into observation instead of action. Once a plan has been researched and thought through, it's time to get into the game. If you agree in advance that the worst thing that can happen is being wrong, big deal. You try something different.

Keeping your eye on the mark is the only way to hit it. You cannot hit a target you aren't focused on unless it's an accident. **Don't trust your success to accidents. Trust your success to yourself and your actions.**

Action and persistence go hand in hand. The more options you have available to you, the more action you can take. Taking action gives you results you can measure, evaluate, and proceed with after modification.

If you wait till you have every piece of the puzzle figured out before you feel confident that you can do it, you'll miss out on the whole journey. Don't get caught in the waiting game and in telling yourself stories about when this or that happens you'll be ready. Those are just self-stalling stories that will leave you with nothing but regret.

All the winners I know take action. Be a person who takes action and you'll never feel ashamed or guilty for not trying and doing.

The most fun is on the playing field. Every professional sports team starts the year focusing on winning the championship. They practice every day with winning in mind. Some days are better than others. They never allow one bad practice or one bad day to deter them from the end result. I suggest that you take on this kind of focus and commitment.

Each day should be dedicated to working your plan to get better and to move closer to your goals. Some time ago, I started calling this kind of focus "oxygen-thinking only," which means that you do only what's absolutely required for the task or mission at hand to get the result. Think Apollo 13, where the astronauts were running out of oxygen and there was no time to waste. All you have is that second to move yourself further toward home. In business, that's exactly how I operate: oxygen-thinking only. All the stuff we don't absolutely have to do right now we don't do. Being efficient is really all about oxygen thinking—and option thinking. You must ask yourself, *What are my options?* You assess all the options, make decisions, then take action.

Throughout this book I've endorsed planning time and again. I'm so insistent about it because most people just don't want to give it the time it deserves; it just seems to be too tedious for them to really take the time to plan. Most people are out in the middle of the ocean with the sails just being battered around, and they're going nowhere. If you take a look at why businesses fail, or why a certain area in a person's life isn't working, it's usually because they haven't put much thought into it. They haven't taken the time to simply ask, "What am I trying to do? What are the different ways I can do it?" Nor have they taken the time to decide which way makes the most sense for them.

You can be different. You can take the time to plan so you're laser-focused on your outcome. Then you're poised for oxygen-thinking only—you're poised to take action on creating the life of your dreams.

### CHAPTER 9

# Visualize and Meditate Your Way to Success

*It is in vain to expect our prayers to be heard, if we do not strive as well as pray.*

*—Aesop*

In 1995, I started to visualize on a regular basis. I read about how athletes and successful entrepreneurs do the same, so I figured why not? I started a visualization board and put it up on my home office wall. Any time I saw a materialistic thing I wanted or trip I wanted to take, I'd get a photo of it and glue it to the board. I'd get all my emotions behind the visualization session I was doing. I'd see myself already enjoying the object I wanted.

In May of 2000, I was sitting in my office at 7:30 A.M. We had recently moved into our new home in Rancho Santa Fe, California, and my son Keenan came in and sat on a couple of boxes that had been in storage for four years. The tape from the moving company was still on all the packages. He asked me what was in the boxes and I tried to explain to him that my vision boards were in there. You can imagine what my five-year-old thought about that: *Dad's vision-whats?*

So I opened them up, and on the first board was a photo of a Mercedes sports car and a watch and so forth (all of which I had already acquired by then). But as I pulled the second board out, I started to cry. You see, on the board was a picture of the house we had just bought and were living in! Not a house like it. *The house.* In that moment, I came face to face with the miracle of creation. Here was tangible confirmation that all I had believed and taught about thoughts moving into physical form was true and right and real.

The house I live in today was a home I had seen and cut out from *Dream Homes* magazine four years earlier. It sits on five and a half acres with spectacular views and has 320 orange trees. I am excited for you to have this same kind of experience—not necessarily of living in a house like mine, but of having your desires manifest into reality, of having what you know intellectually become a visceral encounter with the creative power inside every one of us.

## VIVID VISUALIZATION: FUEL FOR YOUR DREAMS

Most people who achieve their dreams know visualization is one of the key factors. I'm sure you've heard of how Jim Carey, the actor, wrote himself a check for twenty million dollars long before he ever made it in Hollywood. He would visualize himself receiving that amount for a movie. We all know his vision has come true.

One of the most important elements of creation is the ability to see yourself already in possession of the materialistic or physical state you're creating prior to the actual evidence of such. Visualization is the art and discipline of being able to see that which you seek or desire, using your own mental images. In this book, you've already learned several tools for visualization, including the super-effective method of describing what you're creating in detail, putting it in writing, reading it so it can be recorded, then playing that recording for yourself while you picture it all in your mind's eye.

Why does it work? There are a couple of factors at play when you start to visualize. **The first is that you create "cells" of recognition in your brain that, through repetition, become fixed in your psyche.** Once they're fixed in your mind, your subconscious automatically goes to work on the manifestation of what you desire.

You should recall from earlier chapters that when you focus on anything, your vibration is automatically seeking everything else that is in harmony with that vibration and immediately moves toward any corresponding vibration or frequency. The important thing is that you actively put yourself in the vibration you must for your desired outcome to be created.

**Second, focus is power.** Just as you use a magnifying glass to harness the sun's rays and create a fire, you can use visualization to harness the energy you need to create your dreams. The best way to become good at visualization is by practicing. It doesn't come easily to everyone, so don't feel put off if it's not a snap the first time you do it. Once you've practiced enough, however, it will become a habit just like anything else.

For some people, it's so hard to focus on one thing. It's said we have forty to fifty thousand thoughts per day, most of which serve no purpose. Visualization is an excellent way to get control of your mind and focus on what you want.

## VISUALIZATION EXERCISES

In the book *Experiences in Visual Thinking,* author Robert McKim offers many exercises for the "inner eye." One of the most powerful is to simply close your eyes and summon the image of something and then start adding detail until that thing becomes incredibly vivid. This is called sensing with your mind's eye. Take your time and visualize—see, touch, hear, taste, smell with your imagination—the following. Start with the simpler images and work your way up to the more complex ones.

➤ Your childhood bedroom

➤ A familiar face

➤ A galloping horse

➤ A rosebud

➤ A light bulb

➤ The feel of soft fur

➤ The voice of a teacher

➤ An itch

➤ Kicking a can

➤ A potato chip

➤ Toothpaste

➤ Perspiration

➤ Hunger

➤ Washing your hair

➤ A cough

➤ Drawing a circle on a piece of paper

➤ A stone dropped into a quiet pond with concentric ripples forming and expanding outward

➤ These words flying away, high into the blue sky, finally disappearing

➤ Your shoe coming apart in slow motion and each piece drifting away into space

➤ Cutting an orange into five pieces, putting one in your mouth, and arranging the slices on a yellow plate

Another good exercise is to choose an object and stare at it for about thirty seconds. Then close your eyes and see it on the screen of your mind. Try to explore by moving it around, making it bigger or smaller. What does it feel like?

After you've mastered simple images, start to visualize much more complex things that you want to create, no different from a sculptor who must first see her "end result" before she begins to sculpt. **So must you clearly see your end result before it will appear.**

Visualization is your key to creating the mental mold you need for the manifestation of what you desire in physical form. Remember that you're dealing with infinite source and supply. Don't sell yourself short by visualizing what you think you "can" have or create. Just be very specific and precise about what you want. If you're not sure, take the time to think it through.

There are forces at work that are very powerful and can accommodate the grandest of ideas and dreams. Just look around you. Everything you see started with someone saying, "Hey, I wonder if I can do that or have that."

*You can!*

## THE POWER OF THE SOURCE

Meditation is the best known way for tapping into the source of all supply and creation, and for feeling the power of being more connected than ever before to the spiritual essence of our universe and being. It has been practiced in the East for eons, but has only become mainstream in the last fifteen years here in the West, mainly through the teachings of the transcendental meditation approach of Maharishi Mahesh Yogi. Dr. Deepak Chopra is greatly responsible for helping the West grasp the Maharishi's teachings.

More than five million people worldwide practice meditation daily. At least two hundred independent studies have been concluded on the subject, and five hundred scientific studies conducted as well. All the reports indicate a reduction of stress and an increase in creativity and awareness. Numerous physiological benefits as well as psychological ones have been documented and well researched.

Regardless of these studies, in my own experience of meditation, a feeling of timelessness and tranquility is supreme. I can meditate for one hour, and it feels like three minutes. **In this dimension, there's no time as we know it. There's a sense of total connection to the omnipotent source of all that is, and a feeling of oneness with God.** Remember that in chapter 2 you read that people who are able to heal themselves without traditional medical intervention are those who can fall into what Chopra calls "the Gap." Meditation is the best route I know to this great Gap, where you dip directly into the source of all that is.

Most of the time you may feel separated from your source because you're so caught up in the illusion of having a body, which seems to separate you from everything else, as if your skin was some impermeable wall from the rest of the world. This is far from the truth. You're like a wave in the ocean. You may be eight feet off the water but still remain part of the whole. It's your perception of separation that deludes you. Everything in the universe is connected to everything else. When you meditate, you totally change the vibration of every molecule and atom in your body. This allows you to experience a dimension of the universe that's hard to do in everyday life. It's as if you know you're one with the universe. After some practice, there's no doubt that you are.

You don't feel with the physical senses that you need and use to navigate in the external physical world. You feel with the inner and mental senses you have to navigate your inner world.

In the West, people are finally grasping some of the Eastern ways. For someone who has not tried to meditate or research meditation, however, all this may sound odd. And most people tend to dismiss things with which they are unfamiliar.

"Be open to everything and attached to nothing" is a saying I've heard from author and human potential expert Dr. Wayne Dyer. If you have not meditated before, try opening yourself to the possibilities it offers.

## CREATE A TIME OF PEACE

When you take the time to quiet your mind and not allow anything to intrude on your peace, there is stillness in time. You feel suspended in an ocean of tranquility, and all truth seems to stem from this place of inner understanding.

It's the exact opposite place of our rushed, hurried, busy daily lives that we allow to control and stress us. When you meditate you'll find yourself in a place of calm, love, and peacefulness, a place where time is of no consequence and truth is imminent.

It may surprise you that you don't have to learn any special mantras to meditate. You don't need to try any particular method, and in fact I suggest you start with the utterly method-less meditation of simply attending to your breath. Sit quietly and comfortably in a quiet room, then close your eyes. Put all of your awareness on your breathing, and start with a deep and slow breath. Inhale to your diaphragm, feeling your belly expand. Then let the air out slowly. Continue by breathing normally, and stay focused on your breathing. Follow each breath with no thought. If thoughts intrude, just let them pass and bring your attention back to your breath. Your first session might last a grand total of thirty seconds, but you should emerge feeling refreshed and alert. If you can't get thirty seconds with no thought, attempt ten seconds. Next time, try to extend the time further and keep building to longer and longer meditation sessions.

Meditation calms your vibration to the frequency of Creation and Infinite Intelligence. Everything you want in your life comes from this frequency.

You just need to learn a better way to understand the self and acquire an awareness of who and what you really are. From this place of infinite intelligence and knowing, everything is created and everything is possible. All the answers are here.

### CHAPTER 10

# Let Faith Be Your Guide

*So many gods, so many creeds,*
*So many paths that wind and wind,*
*While just the art of being kind*
*Is all the sad world needs.*

—*Ella Wheeler Wilcox*

At seventeen, the young man had a lot to look forward to. He was a talented basketball player and on track to play in the NCAA. He had his future all mapped out: complete college on a scholarship, become a top-notch athlete, and if everything turned out as planned, go on to play pro ball. After all, the scouts were telling him he could have it all.

One Sunday afternoon, he was a passenger in a souped-up car being driven by his buddy as if they were in the Indianapolis 500. They were careening around the perimeter of the shopping center parking lot when, suddenly, the driver lost control of the car. It flipped a few times and landed nose first in a fifteen-foot ditch. To the young man, it all seemed to be happening in slow motion— everything was going so fast that it actually seemed to slow down.

Unharmed, the driver crawled out the rear window and looked back at his nearly unconscious friend, who was obviously hurt. His friend was much larger than he was and would be difficult to lift, much less pull out of that small window. Somehow he did it anyway.

When the boys' parents arrived at the scene, they thought both must be dead. The car was absolutely demolished. Yet they found the boys in the shopping mall; they had wandered in there, bleeding, and were waiting for help on a bench. The police arrived, then the medics, and although the driver had escaped with minor injuries, the passenger was taken to the hospital: The doctors determined he had broken ribs, a broken collarbone, a broken fifth metatarsal, back injuries, and nerve and muscle damage in his left leg.

The boy was scheduled for back surgery and told he would be in bed for at least two months. Then he would have to learn to walk again, slowly. It would be a long time before he could take more than a few steps at a time. He would not be playing basketball anytime soon, if ever again.

Gone was the promise of a scholarship, instantly stripped away like the rubber from squealing tires just hours ago. Six years of intense training would not come to fruition.

Was this young man's life over? He could have felt that way. But a sense of peace had enveloped him as soon as the car started flipping. He was enfolded, mercifully, in faith.

It was the first time he had completely trusted God to take care of him. He was stripped of any illusions of control, and he decided to have faith that everything would work out. He never looked back. He never thought to himself, *I just wish that . . .*

He had no regrets. How can I be so sure? Because that boy was me. This was my first overt lesson in faith, which cemented an attitude I've never since relinquished. It was also my first direct experience of the illusory nature of time. As the car was flipping over, everything slowed down to such a degree that I was able to witness each flip, the trees, the ditch, and the terrified look on my friend's face. Although it happened in seconds, it seemed like a slow-motion movie. It caused a serious curiosity in me about the physical senses and what's real and what's perceived.

## TAKE A CHANCE

You already know that I'm a risk-taker; that willingness to dare comes from my faith. Of course, I believe in doing my best due diligence prior to taking action. When I feel something has merit, I do everything I can to eliminate any potential threat, then I charge forward. There's a belief behind those actions that no matter what happens, it's going to be okay. It may not be to my taste, but everything always works out the way it's supposed to.

If you don't risk money, you can't make a lot of it. If you don't risk your emotions, you can't have a deep, fulfilling relationship. If you don't risk potentially getting injured when you exercise, you don't have the possibility of getting truly healthy. If you don't risk falling short of your dreams, you'll never come close. But are these really risks? Or just acts of faith?

I trust one hundred percent of my being to the universe. I trust life and death to God, so why not everything else?

If you start fearing every day that you're going to die, you won't live. If you focus on failure, you can never succeed. If you fixate on being hurt in a relationship, you can never feel loved. And so on. This just follows the law of attraction: whatever you focus on, you will create. It's so important that you understand and at least try living in accordance with the laws you've learned in this book. I believe in these laws: I don't think they're true, I know they're true. I can come up with example after example after example to illustrate their truth. It's your responsibility, however, not to believe what I say but not to reject it, either. Be open to testing it for yourself. This is an option-thinking book, designed to encourage you to start imagining! *What if this stuff is real? What if it's true? What if the person telling me this stuff has actually done the research and actually tried it—and it works? Maybe it'll work for me.*

I urge you to take this leap of faith with me.

## PUT YOUR FAITH IN THE RIGHT PLACE

Having faith means trusting when you haven't seen the evidence yet. The most important faith you can have is in your Creator, in the Universal Intelligence, in God, no matter what you call your Source.

The complete confidence that everything happens as it is supposed to, and will continue to do so, is the ultimate belief and faith in a higher power. For very specific reasons, humans have been given the ability to choose. Your choices determine your results. Every other creature on Earth has been placed in a very confined and predetermined place. **You, on the other hand, have the ability to co-create your own destiny with the powers given to you.**

To achieve the life of your dreams, you must first have total and undeniable faith—in yourself and in God.

> *If a man could pass through Paradise in a dream, / And have a flower presented to him as a pledge / That his soul had really been there, and if he found / That flower in his hand when he awake— / Aye, what then?*
>
> —Samuel Taylor Coleridge

Not only must you have faith when you're strong, but also it's especially needed when you're feeling down or challenged.

Logical proof does not give rise to faith. Faith comes from the quiet space inside your soul that *knows*. It's that space that speaks to you of greatness and fuller expression and understanding. It comes from looking around and really seeing and listening. It comes from watching a child's innocence, love, and beauty. It comes from love and loving. May you always be blessed with these in your life, for this is the essence of *having it all*.

# About the Author

**JOHN ASSARAF ("The Street Kid")** is best known for being one of the leading optimum performance experts in the world. He is founder of The Street Kid Company, which conducts seminars and coaches senior executives and ambitious entrepreneurs who choose to take their lives and businesses to the next level. An experienced businessman himself, John has owned and operated a franchising company whose annual real estate sales topped three billion dollars. He was also part of the senior executive team who grew Internet virtual tour pioneer Bamboo.com from a team of six people to fifteen hundred in just over a year, netting millions in monthly sales and completing a highly successful NASDAQ IPO.

From his early years as a street gang member to his life today, John has been fascinated with why some people achieve great results in their lifetimes while others merely eke out an existence. As a result, he has spent the last twenty-two years studying peak human performance and behavior and has identified the mental factors that lead to failure or success at the highest level in entrepreneurial endeavors and life.

John lives in Rancho Santa Fe, California, with his two amazing sons, Keenan and Noah. He enjoys reading, writing, consulting with companies, mentoring ambitious entrepreneurs, and nuturing the wonderful relationship he's developed with his sweetheart, Maria.

In his spare time, John loves to ski, travel, exercise, and entertain friends and family. He's also known for his passion and appreciation for excellent wines.

*To learn more, visit the website at www.TheStreetKid.com.*

John Assaraf delivers the powerful strategies and techniques
detailed in *The Street Kid's Guide to Having It All*
to companies and individuals.

For information on speaking, coaching, seminars, and
workshops, contact John at:

**The Street Kid Company**
3525 Del Mar Heights Rd., Suite 356, San Diego, CA 92130
Tel. (858) 759-9527 — Toll-Free (800) 552-3668 — eFax (858) 777-5740
www.TheStreetKid.com

**Special Free Bonus**

Receive a weekly e-newsletter designed to assist you in putting what you've learned from this book into practice! Visit www.TheStreetKid.com to get weekly reminders and step-by-step guidance through the book's exercises and key principles—a $97 value—as our gift to you.